The Life and Death of Rising Star

STEVE IHNAT

Gone Too Soon

Steve Inhat. Photo compliments Ihnat Family Collection

"Steve Ihnat was unique. Quiet would be the leading attribute of his acting. Silence was his power. His gaze was always empowered by his silence. His years of football gave his movement a power and a stealth unmatched. When he broke silence, you listened because that silence gave his words an intensity that babbling would never have. God took him young. I think He feared him."

– Ed Asner
Los Angeles, California

The Life and Death of Rising Star

Rising Star

STEVE IHNAT

Gone Too Soon

by Linda Alexander

BearManor Media

2018

The Life and Death of Rising Star Steve Inhat – Gone Too Soon

© 2018 Linda Alexander

For information, address:

BearManor Media
P. O. Box 71426
Albany, GA 31708

bearmanormedia.com

Typesetting and layout by John Teehan

Published in the USA by BearManor Media

ISBN — 978-1-62933-367-0

Table of Contents

THIS BOOK IS DEDICATED to the memory of two important people in Steve Ihnat's life, two people who have gone on to join him on the other side since work on this book about his life story began.

First, Steve's sister, Emily Ihnat Mordue. He loved his family with abandon. Emily, a wonderful and loving woman, left this world suddenly in June of 2016.

Steve's good and loyal friend, and writing partner, Steve Lodge, died in February 2017 after an extended illness.

Foreword

WHEN HE WAS GROWING UP in Canada, his "moniker" was Ace. When we met during the auditions for *Dragstrip Riot* in 1956, it was just plain Steve. He was funny. A kind of wry, poking funny that just pulled us together. He had already been cast as one of the "bad guys" while I was still auditioning. Steve was vociferous about letting the producer and the director know that I was the one for the part, whatever the part was. It worked. I got the part. I had never had a "best friend" before and I sure as hell couldn't've found anyone better.

Almost immediately Steve and I began discussing our characters and what we could do to make them more real.

His instincts were incredible. He just knew. And those instincts became more and more honed and evidenced through the subsequent five movies we did together.

We became roommates. We struggled, grew, laughed, cried and laughed a lot. We cut our teeth hustling and scuffling around Hollywood looking for work. And Steve was forever growing. I began wondering, "Why is a guy this talented not working ALL the time?" It didn't make sense.

He did plays, he coached friends and acquaintances, he auditioned for everything. And he just kept getting better and better. He worked construction, dug ditches, stocked shelves in markets, and would somehow find ways to incorporate those experiences into his performing.

Early on he had spent considerable time at The Pasadena Playhouse where he nourished his love of Shakespeare. Even I benefitted from the Bard's influence on Steve. He taught me how to fence and the difference between fencing style and rapier style. I think I still have some of the welts to prove it.

Every Steve Ihnat performance was special and left people buzzing about them. Actor, writer, director. Steve was all of them and then some.

God only knows what he would have accomplished had he not shuffled off his mortal coil when he did. It's been 47 years and from time to time I'll catch myself asking, "Now, how would Steve have played this?"

Linda has brilliantly captured all of this and much, much more in her book. Steve was there next to me, pointing out the parts he didn't want me to miss, as I read it.

God bless and keep you, Steve. You are missed.

– Gary Clarke, May 2018

Acknowledgements & Author's Notes

ONE NIGHT A FEW YEARS AGO my husband and I had settled into bed for the night. We were watching television, flipping channels as we tried to find something to lull us to sleep. Suddenly, my eyes popped wide open as I saw a face on the screen, a face I'd seen before. Many times, apparently. I exclaimed with determined certainty, "I know that man!"

The show was *The Outer Limits*. The episode was the first of two segments of "The Inheritors." The actor I was so sure I knew was Steve Ihnat. Of course I didn't know him. There was no way I could know him. I'd never met the man. I was only six years old when that particular episode first aired. Yet the more I watched this fascinating actor on the screen in front of me that night, the more I was determined that somehow I already had him in my consciousness. Somehow and some way.

I'm weird like that. When my mind grabs onto something, or someone, it refuses to let go. So it was with Steve. I couldn't stop thinking about him; he would be my next biography. My mind wouldn't let go of him and in some strange way, he wouldn't let go of me. No question. I'd been looking for someone new to write about, and each time I had considered another individual before this, not a single soul had stuck. Yet... Steve was the one. He was with me and wouldn't go anywhere until I told his story.

Trust me, now I do know Steve, as much as anyone can know someone who is no longer on this earth, someone they've never physically met. I got so much more than I bargained for when I first began researching the life of Steve Ihnat. He was a man of many dreams, amazing determination, more than his share of confidence and talent, and an abundance of love for family and friends and fellow actors. Yet what really gave me the most difficulty in putting his world back together with total honesty was the underlying mystery which followed him throughout his life, and even into the facts surrounding his untimely death. Steve Ihnat was an enigmatic man who left so much of his story untold, a story which, to this day, continues on with so many unanswered questions.

I could never have written this book without all the help offered along the way. It is always an honor to write such an unvarnished personal story, to have family and close friends open their hearts and memory vaults to me. I will not write a biography without two things on my side—the ability to tell the complete truth of the individual's life as best as I can, and truth with compassion. I want nothing more than to show the human side of the individual who was seen on television and movie screens, to show their fans who this person was when the cameras shut off.

I have made a very dear friend thanks to Steve. Sally Ihnat Marshall was the love of his life. Theirs was a true romance for the ages, one of those, "noticed across the room and then together forever" love stories. From our first communication, Sally has trusted me with her memories, writings, photos, and family, and I pray I have done her dear Steve justice.

Gaby Michel is Steve's daughter-of-the-heart. From all accounts, he loved her deeply, and she still loves him. She has graciously shared memories that only a close family member could offer.

In another life, Brenda Mordue-Humphries and I could've been sisters. We connected closely from our very first contact. In fact, however, she is Steve's niece, and memories of her Uncle Steve have enriched his story with a sweet personal depth.

Steve Makaj, Steve's nephew, opened his heart to explain family dynamics, giving great insight into Steve and Sally as parenting role models. He, too, loved and looked up to his Uncle Steve, even being named after him, and becoming an actor in his footsteps.

Wayne Grajeda, Sally's brother, also saw Steve as a successful role model. As his older brother-in-law, Steve was kind and thoughtful, and Wayne looked forward to a growing relationship with him which, sadly, didn't have the chance to happen. He shared memories and photos.

Steve Lodge was a wonderful, loyal friend to Steve. Sadly, he passed away in 2018. He offered me many memories, photos, and source material. I met Steve years ago through another publisher we shared. Little did I know then our paths would cross again. Godspeed, Steve.

One overall description covers actor, Gary Clarke: hysterically funny. There is more to him, however, and as Steve's first friend in Hollywood, he was loyal and like a brother to him. I'm so very grateful to Gary for his friendship and thoughtfulness in sharing his Steve with me.

Ed Asner generously responded almost immediately to my request for an interview. He and his daughter, Liza, thoughtfully gave of their time to help me round out my picture of Steve's early days as an actor. His memories were invaluable.

Clu Gulager's insights offered a wisdom to the memory of Steve's life that proved to be almost prophetic. He had a clear awareness of his friend's talent and character.

Morgan Brittany's recollections came through the eyes of a child, and were very helpful in showing the fatherly side of a man who was incredibly adept at dealing with children, a man who loved kids long before he had his own.

Frank Converse had a bi-coastal friendship with Steve that withstood the test of time. Frank was quick to offer his emotions and thoughts on Steve's intellect and talent.

Ted Mikels expounded on Steve's early years in the industry. He thought highly of his friend and co-worker. Sadly, we lost him in 2016. God bless you, Ted.

Larry Dane was one of Steve's close friends. He kindly offered memories.

Linda Goranson and Grahame Woods not only shared recollections of the last major commercial production of Steve's career, *Strike!*, but took time from their busy schedules to see to it I was able to view that film.

Doug Gurney was of great importance in fitting pieces together of the end of Steve's life. His father was one of the last people to know Steve in France and without Doug's input, crucial details would never have been uncovered.

Sandy Brooks' mother, Joan French, and friend, Irene Chapman, ran Steve's fan club in Canada. Sandy and Joan shared photos and newspaper clippings from the club's archives. They were a fiercely dedicated group who stood by him and became friends, as well as ardent admirers of his career. Sandy facilitated everything the club offered to the book's success, and knew Steve when she was just a child.

A number of Steve's compatriots in the industry were happy to share their memories: Bonnie Scott Armstrong, Rona Barrett, James Drury, Susan Hart, and John Schuck.

Thank you to Dr. Raymond Martinez and son, Vidal, for their correspondence.

Steve Osifchin gave me details about Steve's family background in what was at the time of Steve Ihnat's birth the country of Czechoslovakia. His website, http://www.tccweb.org, "The Carpathian Connection," has extensive information on the people and geography. His help went above and beyond.

Barbara Peterson is a pioneer in Steve Ihnat fandom and should be recognized as such. Her many webpages on him are partially represented at http://volcanoseven.com/BriefCandle/Bio1.html. Thanks to Barbara for being my "Beginners Guide To Steve Ihnat."

Gloria and Wally Rzemienski came to me via the internet after research was underway. Gloria is one of Steve's many cousins and her husband, Wally, an avid genealogist. They were helpful with family history, and Gloria has become a cyberfriend.

Randal Wheeler is a man with excellent taste in classic entertainment, and I call him a friend. He was the first person in cyberspace to champion a book on Steve Ihnat, assuring me that, to paraphrase an old saying, "If I wrote it, they would read." Indeed, Steve's fans are now making themselves known in great numbers.

Bruce Kogan has been a cyberfriend for a while. He has dedicated a lot of time to professionally reviewing those films and television shows of yesteryear.

An author must rely on the kindness of many strangers when doing the research required for a project of this magnitude. Those strangers included: Rachel Bernstein with the Academy of Motion Picture Arts and Sciences' Margaret Herrick Library; Susan Chicoine with The Old Globe Theatre; Melanie Dawn; Miriam Gonzalez, KOLO News; Amy Gould-Pilz; Trudy Hoffman; Wendy Hopkins; Margaret Houghton; C. Courtney Joyner; Omar la Tuee; Juliana Minsky; Chris Poggiali; Michelle Rio; Jeff Simon with The Buffalo News; and Ed Valtenbergs. If I've missed anyone, my apologies. It certainly wasn't intentional.

Last, but never least, I could not have completed this book without input and support of a personal nature. Gerry Purcell of the Wetumpka, Alabama Chamber of Commerce offered me his thoughts when I had questions of a business nature related to Steve's story. Sharon Alexander let me repeatedly bend her ear over issues which threatened to stall completion of the book. She helped me work my way through the roadblocks. Larry Blanks thoughtfully jumped in at the last minute and helped me work out a problem, brilliantly solving it in short order. My cousin, Lou Hansen, will never know how instrumental she was in getting this book to print. Her counsel turned on a lightbulb in my brain that literally brought Steve Ihnat's story full circle and put the missing links into place. I love you, Lou.

And as always, complete gratitude and never-ending love to my husband, Tom, who always puts up with me as I dig into the lives of these fascinating folks of Hollywood… over and over and over.

– Linda Alexander Prevost
Montgomery, Alabama

Prologue

THIS STARTS OUT AS THE STORY of a little boy with oversized dreams, a boy born with the name of Stefan Ihnat. He then became known as Steve, a young man who grew up to become an actor. Not just any run-of-the-mill actor, either, but a highly-recognizable face and name on North American television, as well as in film around the world.

Steve Ihnat was a dramatic actor teetering on the edge of super-stardom. He was an actor whose every known moment, had Fate handed him a kinder script, would have been written about in all the fan magazines, from his early days into his golden years, and he would have been gossiped over ad nauseam on all the talk shows. His life story would eventually have been sealed into the annals of entertainment history. This opinion was shared by many within the industry, according to such well-known superstars of today as Ed Asner, Gary Clarke, and Clu Gulager.

Steve's story isn't an unusual story in and of itself. Many well-known and talented actors have come and gone through Hollywood since its earliest days. His tale, however, is shrouded in mystery. He lived amidst a period in world history which literally kept him company each step of his life, following him around the world, and even onto television and movie screens. The details which led up to his death could not have been more the stuff of a movie script if Steve wrote the story himself. Steve Ihnat starred in his own real-life mystery, one which remains unsolved to this day.

He was a man who knew what he wanted from childhood, someone who never once wavered in his intent to get where he knew he was meant to be in life. He never made a back-up plan because he never intended to need a back-up plan. There was never a single thought in his mind he would do anything else with his life except become a self-sufficient, successful actor.

He did that even though his last name was, at best, difficult to spell, and nearly impossible to pronounce when casting agents saw it on paper, or called him with a job. That name made sure that his Czechoslovakian heritage preceded him before his face was ever seen. Those who doled out the roles of a supposedly make-believe world created for the screen found it an even bigger task to match Steve Ihnat's name with his face.

But, oh, that face! That face became his saving grace, quickly making him well-known in North American entertainment. Those behind the scenes of television—casting directors, directors and producers—discovered that despite the challenge his name might create in finding him in their Rolodex, each time they used him in a production, Steve Ihnat proved his worth, and then some. His acting skills were more than evident, and audiences began wanting to see him again, and again.

Even viewers who hadn't yet caught onto his name but repeatedly caught sight of him on their TV screen, and the majority of them were women, these people would suddenly brighten when they recognized that face. It wasn't long before bona fide fans made it a point to learn and remember who this man was, and they made it a point to know him by name so they could scan their television guide for him every single week. They would pull out their marking pen and circle any featured show with that unusually-spelled name listed as a guest star.

Sometimes there were difficult choices to make. Steve Ihnat quickly became such a busy performer he was seen more than once on any given night, on more than one show. These were the years before shows could be recorded, and usually only one television set was owned in each household. His resume filled up fast and in but a few years, he became of the busiest character actor guest stars on television. Soon, he veered off into television movies, and then on to the big screen, while never forsaking his small screen fans. He worked simultaneously in television and film, and then found himself doing even more, sidelining behind the scenes on the film set. He was on his way, almost seamlessly adding "writer, director, and producer" to his already-full resume.

Sadly, in the midst of a career on the fast track to make Steve Ihnat one of those names which could never be forgotten despite the passage of time, he was ripped away from the world of entertainment. At a young age, he died while on a trip to Cannes, France, reportedly from a heart attack.

Steve Ihnat died alone. He was in Cannes to attend the Cannes Film Festival, working on distribution opportunities for a movie he made titled *Do Not Throw Cushions Into the Ring* (1970). Just prior to leaving the

United States for the trip, he was cleared by a physician, and declared to be in excellent health. Yet suddenly, he was dead, and the world would never get the chance to appreciate the full body of his artistic potential.

As his stepdaughter, Gaby, said about this man she called her beloved Daddy Steve, "You don't have to know him to enjoy a story about coming from nothing, making your dreams come true, gaining the respect and admiration of your peers, finding the love of your life, creating a family and dying at the most prestigious film festival, all by the age of thirty-seven."

This is the story of a little boy who grew into a youngster who became quite the man, an actor who unquestionably left his mark on the world of entertainment history. This is the story of Steve Ihnat, a rising star who died far too soon.

This is also a multi-layered love story ... between a man and a woman; and between a man and his children—first, a little girl he never knew he needed in his life until she became his daughter; then, an infant boy whose birth thoroughly awed him, a miraculous act beyond anything he had ever experienced, or any part he ever played on a make-believe stage.

This is a traditional celebrity biography on one hand, but it reads in an untraditional fashion. Steve's story is a cautionary tale of Hollywood, its pitfalls, struggles, and outrageous highs and lows.

Yet in the end, this is most certainly a deep and troubling mystery story, a mystery which endures, a mystery which even today stars rising star, Steve Ihnat, in his greatest role. Ever.

Chapter One

ON THE 7ᵀᴴ OF AUGUST, 1935, a baby boy, Stefan, was born to Andrej and Maria Ihnat, reportedly in a thatched hut with a dirt floor in Jastrabie, near Michalovciach, Czechoslovakia. Theirs was a poor, tiny town, surrounded by forests and meadows, and there are questions as to how well his parents were able to take care of their family. In some reports, resources were limited at best. Other information has indicated his father had enough money to keep his kids clothed and fed.

In either case, they did the best they could with what they had. Living conditions in their part of the world at that point in history were less than desirable, and baby Stefan was bitten on the ear by a rat. There was no way to keep rodents out of their living area despite regular efforts. Stefan's older sister may have attended the small local school, an establishment which was in session only during the winter. All children from a very young age were expected to work in the fields in the summertime.

World War II loomed large in the lives of the Ihnat family long before the birth of Stefan. Their country, Czechoslovakia, was on the verge of falling in desperation to Hitler before the baby was even four years old. The family escaped their country and on March 11, 1939, about three days before the country was declared to be under "executive power" of Hitler's army, four-year old Stefan, his parents, a brother, Vincent, and sister, Susan, managed to gain passage on the last available boat bound for Canada via New York. They settled in the town of Lynden, in Ontario, and slowly learned how to build a new life, a life which provided them so much more promise.

The growing little boy became known as Steve in this English-speaking country. He probably would have followed the same path his father walked, becoming an honest, hard-working dairy farmer, except such a

Baby Steve, Sister Sue, and grandmother outside home in Czechoslovakia;
photo compliments Brenda Mordue-Humphries

life never suited him. Somehow, even as a small child, he had it in his head
that he wanted to do something far-reaching, beyond the simple life into
which he was born. Young Steve held high, complicated expectations for
himself.

The *Antonia*, ship which brought the Ihnat family to North America

Nonetheless, as he grew older, he didn't really rebel, at least not out-wardly. His older brother, Vincent, died in a tragic accident and so, for many years, his family had no idea Steve wasn't looking toward the day when, as the oldest living son, he would inherit the family farm. He duti-fully did his share of the daily chores—bringing in the crops, baling the hay, thrashing wheat and oats, and, with his mother, taking their home-raised produce to sell at the local market.

He never complained or shirked his responsibilities yet his mind was usually elsewhere. One of his many tasks was to take the grapes grown on their farm and see that they were sold, and he always did what was expect-ed of him. Always. With each passing day, with each job, and as his body strengthened and matured with all the physically hard work he under-took, he looked ahead to find that one opportunity which would take him well beyond the confines of his limited small-town life. He knew there was more out there for him. There was a bigger world. He was convinced he was meant to do so much more with his life. Lynden was a nice place to grow up but it was too small-town for the high-dreaming Steve Ihnat.

None of Steve's family arrived in North America with any knowledge of the English language. At a young age Steve and his sister learned enough to speak and write, and they were immersed in the English-speaking cul-ture of the Lynden school system. Another child, Emily, had been born since they moved to Canada. She was still a baby, and English would be her natural language outside the home.

Ihnat farmhouse, Lyndon, Ontario, Canada

The kids made friends, and Steve interacted with people at the market as he helped his mother sell homegrown products. Even at this young age, before he was a decade old, he was working the farm, he was competent, and fully aware of what was expected of him. His parents knew just enough of the language to get by and they needed their kids to help them communicate. Their native language was always spoken amongst the family.

* * *

A few years later, Steve went to the United States with his mother, visiting a cousin named Mike Bosko. Her family, whose name in the Old Country was Buskova, came to North America and settled in New Jersey, as had her husband's brothers and his wife and children. This is likely the first time Steve ever entered the States except for docking in New York when they left Czechoslovakia. He was five feet tall, and one of his sisters made the trip with them. They stayed for about a month.

By his early teen years, Steve still had his sights set on an occupation he expected would transport him far beyond the confines of his hometown of Lynden. Years later as an adult he remembered those earliest days on the farm as he kept his eyes on something much different. About his daring, lofty aspirations, he said, "I think wanting to act started when I was about 14 as an escape valve to my environment. I… decided I wanted to be everything in life. Acting is the best way to do it."

He always had tunnel-vision. He took care of the jobs required of him by his parents while his mind stayed focused far ahead on his dream. It was his regular practice to dramatically spout Shakespeare at the top of his lungs as he rode the tractor. His words, "As I worked in the fields I found myself… memorizing plays in which I played all the parts. I had plenty of open space in which to train my voice, and since I was all alone, I could pantomime and ham it up to my heart's content." When he would get ready for bed in the evenings, he'd stand in front of the mirror and play out his own imaginary scenarios.

Steve and his sisters, and friends, had the great outdoors of Lynden in which to roam, sledding down the hills at the back of their property in the frigid cold of the Canadian winter, and riding bikes and getting muddy and dirty in the streams in the warmer seasons. Lynden was a sleepy, friendly community of mostly farmers whose kids invented their own amusements most of the time, and there were wide open spaces for them to do exactly that.

Ihnat farm outhouse, Lyndon, Ontario, Canada

Ihnat farm barn, Lyndon, Ontario, Canada

An outhouse, built by Steve's dad, served to take care of personal needs while the family was in the thick of their daily routines of work and play. A dense grove of trees at the back of their land gave the kids all sorts of places to hide and create imaginary scenarios. Steve's father also built a large barn in back of the main house. Besides providing a practical home for their farm animals and the crops they took in, it served as a perfect place for youngsters to engage in hide-and-seek, sneak a kiss, expand their imagination, and while away their free time. An exterior wall of the barn, years later, showed where many had etched their names or initials, or the young loves of a number of generations past.

Steve played football in his middle school years, an occupation which might have had the power to remove him from his adolescent reality and bring about a new, more exciting one. After about six or so months of playing halfback for the Hamilton Junior Tiger-Cats Football Club, he was forced to give up the sport due to a significant injury. Sports proved to not be his ticket out of his small town life.

A few years later, Steve won a drafting scholarship to Westdale Collegiate in Hamilton, just a short trip away, and he finished out his high school years in "the big city." Going to school every day in Hamilton, leaving the small-town atmosphere of Lyndon for the nearby bustling business center, where there was activity far beyond farming to attract the teenager, helped solidify his desire to depart from the slow, quiet country climate. He would do something more intellectual with his life beyond the farm. There was now no doubt in his mind.

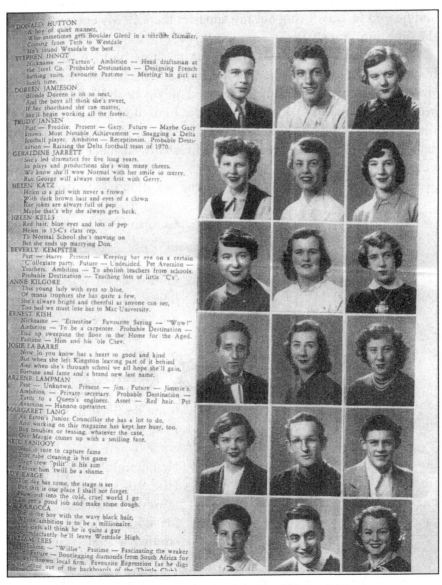

Steve Ihnat's senior year high school yearbook photo, La Raconteur, Westdale Collegiate, Hamilton, Ontario, Canada

There wasn't a moment when that urge to act ever left him. With each passing year, he still stood in front of his mirror every chance he got and performed scenes from plays, or created his own. He began writing snippets of scenes. He would carefully listen for all sorts of accents when he was out in public, and then mimic them when he was by himself, reciting dialogue in every dialect he could come upon. Steve Ihnat was single-minded and focused to a fault. He went to the movies every chance he got, and he said he was "living out my fantasies there…. My environment at the time didn't satisfy me."

When he finally finished his last year in school, his high school yearbook indicated his nickname was "Tarzan," and his favorite pastime was "meeting his girl at lunch time." Steve had only gone to Westdale for one year yet he managed to cement a place for himself in a short amount of time, clearly becoming comfortable among the other students and fitting right in, with them accepting him wholeheartedly. He made friends without any difficulty.

His senior photo blurb stated his true ambition was to become the

Steve in 1954 with his sisters Susan and Emily; photo compliments Brenda Mordue-Humphries

"head draftsman at the Steel Company" but he would probably end up "designing French bathing suits." Much of this detail was pure silliness as was expected of graduating seniors. If one were to base his aspirations on nothing more than what was written in his yearbook, it would have shown Steve to be destined to little more than the norm for the average young man living in Hamilton, Ontario, Canada. His professional intentions, however, went far beyond his hometown, beyond becoming a draftsman in his comfortable world, even beyond the country in which he lived, but he wasn't yet ready to publicly announce this insistent, nagging call he felt to be on the international stage and to become a name known to many.

He felt as if he had to pay homage to drafting as a formal occupation for the sake of his hardworking parents who did everything they did for their children. After all, he went to Hamilton on a drafting scholarship to satisfy his family. Instead, the change in schools served to enhance his dissatisfaction with what his parents wanted out of him, and also with where his life was clearly headed if he didn't change the course it was on. And soon.

* * *

By utilizing the scholarship to its fullest potential, Steve figured out that his family would get student tax benefits from the government for his schooling while, at the same time, he could buy himself extra time to plan his next steps. This proved to benefit his parents, as well as him, and the analytical and careful examination of his life's path led him first to a job with Ontario Hydro as a draftsman. He needed money if he wanted to make these changes. Taking the job padded his wallet and built up his savings to make his travel to California, the place where dreaming about being a professional actor could be turned into a reality.

All this while, never once did he give up. On the contrary. He was carefully making these preparations. His every move was well-considered. He even used some of the salary he received to take night courses in theater arts. He enrolled at the Players' Guild of Hamilton to seriously learn the craft. His sister said he and a friend made a trip to Hollywood during this time. He wanted to test the waters and learn the lay of the land. It was a quick jaunt, just a visit to see what the place was all about. Steve loved it. He was hooked.

In 1956, back in Canada, he got a break. Those acting lessons with the Players' Guild paid off and he was cast in the part of Tony Abbott in *Heaven Can Wait*, a play put on at the Guild. This was Steve's first official acting job and if he hadn't already been in love with the whole idea, winning this role in a stage production made it official. The experience brought about the realization that this was a life he could not live without, and he wanted more of it. "I knew this was the only thing I wanted to do with my life."

His name was in the paper with the tag, "newcomer." His picture was featured, as well. The play was put on at his alma mater for three consecutive nights. Steve had a leading role, not a bad deal for his stage debut.

In later years, A. C. Mullock, a member of the Players' Guild staff who eventually went on to become the honorary President, spoke of Steve. He met Steve at an Open House and told him about the "Heaven Can Wait" casting call. "I'd never met a person more set and determined that he was going to become someone, stage-wise," Mullock said about Steve.

Mullock remembered him as a young man with a clearly defined plan for himself. "He had a tremendous drive and he worked like a fool. His English wasn't very good and I had a recording machine. He used to come out here on his way home from work and read his part over and then listen to it. He just worked fanatically, no matter what happened. He was 100 percent dedicated to what he was doing."

It wasn't long after, in an almost immediate turnaround, when Steve finalized his idea to move away from Canada for good, to make the separation from the life he'd always known. His parents were not happy with his decision. They were always certain he would grow out of this idea. They counted on their belief that he would never leave them, and in due time he would settle down to run the one hundred-acre Ihnat family farm. In later years, he told a reporter, "This was a real close-knit European family, and when I tried to tell them I wanted to act instead of taking over the farm, Mom and Dad literally thought I was crazy."

Steve had only $900 in his pocket and no promise of work on the other end but, determinedly, he made a permanent move to the United States despite the deep disappointment to his parents and sisters. Canada had recently experienced a political upheaval with the election of a Prime Minister from the Progressive Conservative Party for the first time since 1935. The moment was as good as any in Steve's eyes. "The reason I left home so young was not any kind of anti-Canada feelings. I just knew I had to get far away from my parents if I was going to get my career started without constant battles."

Steve Ihnat landed in Los Angeles on a student visa, as a Czechoslovakian citizen previously residing in Canada, with nearly-empty pockets and nowhere to live. Yet as far as he was concerned, life was wonderful.

He was only in his early twenties but he was certain about what he wanted out of life. He started out as a pauper, working at many odd jobs to support himself. "One thing I had going for me in the survival struggle was that I used to trim trees for the lands and forests department [in Canada]. There's a real shortage of skilled gardeners in Southern California and the hourly rates homeowners will pay is fantastic." Steve made plans to take classes at the Pasadena Playhouse before he left Canada for Los

Angeles. Steve's tree-trimming skills proved to be a life saver and in short order he had such well-known customers as Rosalind Russell and Carl Reiner. Others followed.

None of them seemed to mind that Steve had to secure jobs where payment went unreported to the government because of his then-visiting student status in the United States. A few months after his arrival, Lady Luck tapped him on the shoulder.

"The first time I checked with the immigration department in L.A.," he told a reporter, "they said they didn't have any Czechoslovakia quota openings and I didn't qualify as a Canadian citizen. But then they phoned me out of the blue to say they had found two extra Czech quotas and did I want one? I sure did." It is unknown why, after living in Canada for nearly twenty years, he had not become a citizen.

Steve Ihnat came into the country at a difficult time for someone born in the Eastern Hemisphere. For him to attempt to become a legal resident of the United States in 1952, his personal history would have been scrutinized. This was the early days of the Cold War. Just a few years earlier, the Immigration and Nationality Act, otherwise known as the McCarran-Walter Act, had been passed, integrating a number of different laws governing who could, and could not, come into the United States and either live, or stay.

There were a large number of refugees left in Europe as a result of World War II, people still desperately wanting to flee to a better life. The United States government believed there could be a threat from communist infiltrators and laws put in place reflected this concern. A quota system was utilized based on country of origin, with stringent numbers of people allowed in to the United States each year from the restricted Eastern Hemisphere. These numbers were doled out month by month by the Immigration and Naturalization Service (INS).

The McCarran-Walter Act did establish a preference

Steve's visa/passport which he carried in his wallet for the rest of his life

Young Gary Clarke with Steve in the background

for skilled workers who intended to become permanent resident aliens. Steve's plan was exactly that, possibly to eventually become a full-fledged American citizen. He proved himself to be an able-bodied, intelligent young man, likely a productive addition to the fabric of the society of the United States, and was welcomed into the country. He had been a resident of North America for most of his life, a fact which likely cemented his legitimate intent.

Steve's study with the Pasadena Playhouse helped him get small guest roles on television in his early days. Out of the $900 with which he arrived in Hollywood, about $700 went directly and immediately into acting lessons. He followed through with his original plan when he got to California by building upon the acting class credits from the night courses he'd taken with the Players' Guild in Hamilton. This experience allowed him acceptance into the Pasadena Playhouse. Not only did he find himself immersed in learning acting techniques but also different ways of dialogue and dialect, facial expressions, how to stand and walk and talk, and even how to fence.

The Playhouse proved to be more than just a starting place for Steve's career. It introduced him to one of his longest-lasting friendships, a relationship which remained close through to the end of his life. He and Gary Clarke clicked as if they had known each other forever. They were two young men, both single, struggling actors, determined to make it big. Both had a sense of humor which complimented the other, bawdy and fun loving, and sometimes, downright outrageous.

Gary explained how they met. He was doing theater work in Glendale, and an agent named Byron Griffith was in the audience. He was impressed and asked him to do some scenes for him and decided to help Gary get work. Another of Griffith's clients was Connie Stevens, with whom Gary did his first read-through.

He got a call from Griffith one day, telling him about a teen movie in pre-production, and he could probably get him a part as one of the good guy gang members. Did he want it? Gary did what he had to do to get to the audition and he secured the role. The next day Griffith called back to tell him the production lost the lead actor, and did he want to take on that part instead? *Hell, yeah!* Once again, Gary made his way to the set, again had to audition and, in fact, auditioned for five days straight, after which he was finally awarded the role.

It just so happened Steve Ihnat was also agented by Byron Griffith and was sent to the same audition. He had already won the part of the bad guy, so he was on the set during those days as Gary read for his new leading bit. Gary said Steve would sit there and watch him, and encourage him. Connie, who had also been given a part, urged him on, as well. The three of them began forging their longstanding friendship.

Gary saw a lot of talent in his new buddy, this Czech-turned-Canadian-turned-United States resident. They ultimately found an apartment and moved in—going for casting calls together, chasing girls together, always laughing and honing their craft together. They were constantly telling jokes, and pulling jokes on one another. Gary remembered Steve was a master at ad libs and could make up a story on the spot. He could pull off almost any accent, able to listen and faultlessly copy the sound and tone. Gary often heard him talk to his family in their native Czech, noting Steve could slip in and out of a comfortable native accent seemingly without conscious thought.

Gary's family lived in Los Angeles, and Steve became a regular at his mother's dinner table, along with Gary's brothers, Pete and Mike. She adored him and she called him Steve Ignats. He and Gary always had empty pockets, so being fed by his mother was almost part of daily life for the guys. They'd stroll in her door and say in unison, "We're broke. What's for dinner, Mom?"

Or they would find other ways to be fed by Gary's family. His grandfather was an extraordinary cook. He loved to barbecue and Steve could be found at their table eating short ribs during any given family get-together, along with his parents, cousins, Pat and Delores, and his brothers. Steve was just another member of the clan as far as they were concerned, just another son.

Gary and Steve did some other things, too, some of which they weren't always very proud. Still, Gary couldn't help finding humor in the memory. When they first started living together, they shared an old two-story house in mid-Hollywood with O'Dale Ireland, known as Dale. The house was rent-free for them. The owner just wanted bodies in it so it would not stand empty and possibly be vandalized. The three young men had little money between them at any one time and they got creative or, as Gary said, they would not have eaten.

Gary recalled how they often procured their dinner. "We pooled our money," he said. "Sometimes $1.50. We'd go to Ralph's Market wearing big jackets. Maybe I'd get the meat… three filet mignons. That would be about twenty bucks. I'd stuff them in my shirt. Steve got the veggies. Then dessert… all that went under his jacket. Dale, our other roommate, got the cigarettes. He stuck those in his pocket." Gary laughed. "That was in the day of the tight bell-bottom fad. His pants were so tight you could tell his religion."

They paid for milk and bread and walked out of the store. They did this regularly and, somehow, managed to never get caught. They'd take their feast to their empty house—no furniture, just cots to sleep on—and fix their dinner. This was the life for the bachelors, three struggling young actors.

Chapter Two

TELEVISION CAME CALLING FOR STEVE somewhere between 1958 and 1959 on a show called *Traffic Court*. The "plot" was scripted only in terms of an outline, usually about three to four paragraphs of actual case material. The actors took on the role assigned to them from the outline in what was called "planned realism." They usually went through one fast rehearsal about two hours before filming began, with one more rehearsal in front of the rolling cameras. Finally, they went on in front of the cameras again, this time live, and that was beamed out to eager viewers in living rooms across the country.

All of the cast except for the judge, bailiff, and a few other players were "either non-professional or 'new face' actors." There could always be a hitch in the way the show ended up, and this was a testament to how well the non-experienced actor was usually able to handle his or her job. This proved to be an early example of Steve's ability to improvise without benefit of a structured script, something he would do more and more of as his career progressed. The judge was known to regularly change his ruling from rehearsal to air time when something the actor said—ad lib, of course—altered his originally intended ruling. This show paved the way as one of the earliest productions of the "courtroom drama" genre on TV.

About this time, Steve decided to cut his ties with the Pasadena Playhouse. He was no longer able to keep up with the expense of ongoing lessons. As well, he was beginning to find their approach "too academic" for his personal style of acting. He learned a great deal there and was grateful for the experience but he felt it was time for him to move on.

An opportunity came his way which may have spurned on his decision to give up his formal acting classes. Steve was interviewed by Lucille Ball for a contract with the Desilu television studio. The contract would've meant regular roles with the studio, as well as a place in a travelling company under consideration by Desilu. The studio was branching out and making efforts to find new venues. This potentially big break for Steve, however, never came to fruition.

Instead, he and Gary found roles together in a movie titled *Strike Me Deadly* (1963). The originator, Ted V. Mikels, was from Bend, Oregon, and was himself new to filmmaking. Mikels wanted to make a movie he was then calling *Crosshairs*. Ultimately the title was changed because Hollywood couldn't get behind the original and it became his first completed production. Ted went on to become something of a self-starter in the world of horror and schlock movies, making a big name for himself as a B-grade moviemaker.

He had no film experience when he started work on *Strike Me Deadly* but that didn't tamper his exuberance. The storyline had Gary as a newly married forest ranger, taking his bride, Jeannine Riley, on a pseudo-honeymoon amongst the trees in a cabin owned by the Forestry Department. Jeannine Riley had not yet been thought of as a sweet young thing on TV's *Pettitcoat Junction*, a role which would ultimately make her name known to television viewers.

The storied lovebirds had their honeymoon ruined when they witnessed a murder in the remote woods and were hunted down and terrorized by the killer... played by Steve. He filled the role with desperate menace. Even though he was acting opposite his best friend, he, and Gary, were quite believable in their parts as two men at odds with each other. Gary said there were many ad-libs which made their way into the final cut of the movie.

Steve was said to have displayed "great remorse and confusion" and turned his part as a madman into a "sympathetic character." A review said he was "the real powerhouse of this picture." He used a stage name and showed up as Steve Quinn in the credits. At this early point in his career, Steve was concerned about how difficult it was to pronounce and, even more, remember his last name. He wasn't certain the ethnicity of Ihnat would play well in Hollywood.

Ted Mikels said a lot of complimentary things about Steve. "I love Steve and he was so ready and willing to help in every way possible when I was making *Strike Me Deadly* up in Oregon in 1960. I met Steve through Basil (Brad) Bradbury and Gary Clarke...." Bradbury, also from Bend, went on to work as a producer, director, director of photography and editor in the motion picture industry in Hollywood for more than thirty years. He also worked on Steve's last film, *Do Not Throw Cushions Into The Ring*.

Ted went on, "I had transported a huge Mitchell camera… to use it in the backwoods of central Oregon, including hauling that huge beast of a camera up the cricketer stairs to the top of the forest service lookout towers where we filmed from their interiors. Steve was a most willing person to help in all of those heavy-duty chores…."

Steve came up with ideas for the story which Ted thought were good, so he allowed Steve to help him write the script. Ultimately, he ended up writing so much he received a co-credit, listed as Stefan Ihnat, his first official writing credit. Ted explained, "Steve was very diligent in asking me to include some of his thoughts in the screenplay and some dialogue in certain places. Normally I would not allow an actor to do very much of this but Steve was very special and a great talent and everything that he suggested made sense to me so we utilized many of his thoughts…. Anytime Steve would write out something he thought could work, he would bring it to me for approval and most of the time they were good suggestions.

"As a performer he was top notch [sic], incredibly believable and was a wonderful bad guy…. He was quite intense… and was a talent that I really appreciated having with me in the movie. We kept in touch after the movie and I went to see him in a couple of stage plays in which he performed and/or directed and as always he was great. I have often wished I could have Steve with me on movies that I had made since…. He most certainly was a great talent."

The movie was filmed on location in the mountainous woods of Oregon in black-and-white. The decision to not use color was a monetary

A menacing Steve in *Strike Me Deadly*

Steve's first noted television role on *Mike Hammer*

one. The entire production was completed on a fifteen-thousand dollar budget. Gary well-remembered the experience. Ted had a whole passel of kids, six to eight of them was his best recollection. Ted would feed and take care of all of his family, as well as the film crew. He and his bunch lived in a small house, and he would bring all of his neighbors out to meet the "big stars from Hollywood," Gary laughed. Those "big stars" were him and Steve.

*   *   *

Not long after, in Steve's first "official" television role, in 1958, he played a "notorious crook" on trial in "Jury of One," from *Mike Hammer*, the show considered then by some critics to be "the worst piece of sadistic junk" on the tube. The simplistic plot was listed as, "One juror blocks an otherwise unanimous verdict of guilty at the trial of a known crook." Steve's character didn't warrant a name in the credits.

He was picking up any and every possible acting job he could. Taking on live theater, he was cast in a play at the Glendale Center Theater. *Love Comes in Many Colors* was a brand new offering written by husband and wife team, Ruth and Nathan Hale. They founded the theater eleven years earlier. In plays written by the Hales, characters rarely drank, smoked, swore, or did anything worse. Such behavior went against their Mormon faith. Yet their "clean" entertainment offerings seemed to be much in demand, and their theater seats were filled nearly every showing for all the plays they put on.

This was a non-equity job for Steve, as well as all the other actors in the cast, which included Gary Clarke, and starred a sweet young lady named Diane McBain, barely seventeen years old. Diane eventually became an experienced television actress but at this point, just like the rest of Steve's cast mates, they were all acting in *Love Comes in Many Colors* for free. Ruth Hale's explanation for operating this way was, "… we kept our prices low. Others paid actors and went broke. And we train people. We don't have a school but as Ethel Barrymore said, 'The best way to learn to act is to act.' So we mix experienced people with inexperienced and their game improves, like in tennis."

Steve was definitely getting experience, and he wasn't missing a single chance to do so. That month, he achieved another first, his very first movie to show up in theaters, in the forgettable film, *Dragstrip Riot* (1958). While he took on *Strike Me Deadly* first, that film hadn't yet arrived on the screen, ultimately taking four years to come to the public's attention.

Dragstrip Riot was written by George Hodgins and initially directed by David Bradley, whom Gary said was "an idiot." Bradley lasted on the set all of a week. Another director was brought in who wasn't there long enough for Gary to remember his name. From then on, O'Dale Ireland, aka Dale, and officially the producer, played the part of the director. Gary said this was funny because Dale was no director, and the actors actually began to direct themselves.

Gary called *Dragstrip Riot*, "probably one of the worst movies ever made in America." The simplistic plot centered on a young man who promised his mother he wouldn't get into any more fights. He couldn't

Steve as a tough guy, with Gary in his grip, in *Dragstrip Riot*

keep the promise, though, when a motorcycle gang harassed his drag-racing friends and of course, fights ensued. One of the cyclists ended up over a cliff, and Gary's character, the "innocent" young man of the bunch, was blamed.

Steve played Dutch, a menacing troublemaker, leader of a band of greasy motorcycle riders. Good friend-in-real-life, Gary, was the clean-cut guy in the middle of all the trouble Steve's character seemed to cause. The two of them, living together, worked their parts to the hilt. They studied at night, and went at it during the day. Another memorable, known actor in the cast was Connie Stevens, who also sang on the soundtrack. As well, in a role some thirty-five years after she started in films, Fay Wray of *King Kong* fame played Gary's beleaguered mother.

Dale had some creative ideas about moviemaking. A young man by the name of Kuldip Singh from Pakistan had recently appeared on *The Groucho Marx Show* in hopes of earning money to attend UCLA. He did, and Groucho also asked him to sing. He did that, as well. His voice was good, and he ended up with a recording contract and a song heard on the radio, "Woman in Love." He was also signed by Dale to what was then called *Teen-Age Rumble*. He never received any credit for work on the film so whatever Dale saw in him didn't pan out and he ended there just as fast as he began. He did have a few music and acting credits in the late 1950s so he was able to parlay his bit with Groucho into his personal fifteen minutes of fame.

Steve tested for, and won, the part of Dutch. He had a personal habit of often sticking his fingers into his turtle neck sweater and pulling down on it, a quirk which fit in well with Dutch's personality, which helped him snag the role during his audition.

Gary was next to read for his part, and he entered the room. Connie Stevens was already in the part of a girl named Marge. Gary's hair was then a natural sandy, light brown but his new friends thought he needed to be a blond for this role. They convinced him that bright blond hair would best fit the part of this clean-cut character. Gary's sister was a beautician, so the night before, he'd gone to her and she bleached his hair a shining yellow-blond.

The three of them marched up to the producer. Steve went to bat for his new friend, explaining how Gary's now-blond hair made him the perfect candidate for this role. With both Connie and Steve already in the cast, this gave Gary an edge or, as he said, maybe it was just that he was willing to do "anything," but he did secure the male lead, Rick Martin.

Gary Clarke in his new blond hairdo, with Yvonne Lime in *Dragstrip Riot*

Setting the stage for what would become the norm for the rest of Steve's career, and Gary's, Steve played the bad guy, with Gary taking on the role of the clean-cut, innocent good guy.

"After one day's shooting, Steve decided we were going to take the bikes home 'to practice.' We're riding Triumphs. We were on a road that ran from the Valley to the beach, doing about 50. Steve was ahead of me and his bike was shaking. I'm watching, I'm maybe 20 yards behind," Gary explained.

"He can't stop, and the bike keeps shaking more and more. He loses it and slides for I don't know how far. He gets up, and looks okay. But he's scraped all the skin off his kneecap down to his bone. An ambulance took him to the local hospital. The knee was cleaned out with a heavy brush. The skin was grabbed from around his kneecap and they tied a string around it, like a blown-up balloon with stitches. He also took the skin off his knuckles. He had a big gold ring that saved part of his knuckles."

The next day, they were back at work, Steve included, shooting at Paradise Cove. During a scene, Gary walked in the moonlight with an actress named Yvonne Lime, who played his girlfriend, Janet Pearson, and

Steve was seen as part of the action. Toward the end of the shooting, Steve was stooped down, hiding behind a bush. The script called for him to get up and walk away.

Gary said, "He couldn't bend his leg. He was stiff-legged but he never complained. You could see him hobbling out."

Dale, the producer, initially told the cast that filming would take three weeks. They all got their Screen Actors Guild (SAG) cards for this job. According to Gary, after shooting for those first three weeks, they were nowhere near finished. Dale then made them another promise. "If you guys help me out you'll all be stars. This thing is really coming together." A lot of hot air on Dale's part but the truth was… the guys had no other work so they went on with the job. They hadn't been paid and wouldn't see any money for some time. The entire production was non-union and if the union were to catch up with them, they would have all been in big trouble. Gary guessed they went on this way for probably six months, working until they finally did finish.

He remembered Dale "knew how to raise a few bucks" but knew very little about the art of making a film. Still, he was a lot of fun and a great guy. He and Dale and Steve got along famously off the set as well as on, and once the movie action was wrapped, the three of them once again roomed together.

Dragstrip Riot was tagged in the media to be "murder at 120 miles per hour" and hit drive-ins about May, playing off-and-on throughout the year. There was often a double bill with *The Cool and The Crazy* (1958), a film said to be "teenagers on a rampage of violence." Many adults denounced these horrific teen-age-directed movies, bemoaning their popularity with the kids of the day as a strong commentary on the declining state of the younger generation. Clearly these were not Academy Award contenders.

A newspaper clipping gave him some press during the same time frame, announcing "Steve Ihnat, a native Czechoslovakian, who appears in Trans-World's *Teen-Age Rumble*, has applied for U. S. citizenship." *Teen-Age Rumble* was the original title for *Dragstrip Riot*. As for Steve's U. S. citizenship, he never completed the naturalization process. This was another curiosity as to his actual citizenship, however. He was a "native Czechoslovakian," according to this newspaper piece. The clipping, however, gave no mention of his longstanding Canadian residency, and lends credibility to the belief he never became a citizen of Canada.

That year, 1958, he had somewhere in the neighborhood of five seconds of television air time on a show called *Flight*, in an episode titled, "The Derelict." *Flight* was hosted by General George C. Kenney, who was in charge of the United States Army Air Force in the southwest Pacific during World War II. There was a sense of realism to this show, with actual airplane footage interspersed into the studio-filmed sections. Steve's part was so miniscule as to be easily missed but it did count as a credit on his slowly-growing resume.

He was nothing if not determined to try anything and everything to find his way in the industry. He even considered Broadway, taking a break to fly out to New York "to look the place over." Since he had some experience at this point with the acting scene on the West Coast, he felt self-assured. "I think I'm ready for Broadway, and I know I can do it." As conceited as that may have sounded, and he knew it did, he explained, "Where personalities are concerned in this business you have to become self-centered a bit. Not to the point of becoming egotistical but an actor has to be prepared to devote most of his time to his own activities to get anywhere."

It wasn't long, though, before Steve was back in California, plying his trade in Hollywood. Broadway proved not to be for him. He found more success on the screen when he secured a role in "Cargo Hijack," an episode of *Highway Patrol*, which starred Broderick Crawford. He had a featured part as a shady truck driver involved with the owners of a company which fronted an import business. Their real business was in stolen merchandise. Steve's character agreed to have his load stolen in exchange for extra payment as he pretended to be the innocent victim. This was one of his earliest bad guy roles and, as a featured player, may just have helped show casting directors how well he could pull off such a character.

*   *   *

Steve still lived with Gary, and now Dale Ireland was with them. Steve had a steady girl, Jackie Ebeier, and things seemed to be going well for him. He was the sort who wanted his world to move forward fast. He had little patience for inactivity when he had a plan, and Steve Ihnat always had a plan. He knew what he wanted in life, had known ever since he was a boy, and he did what he had to do to put his intentions in place. So far, he was on the right track but even so, Steve was not satisfied to let things coast. He didn't feel as if he were getting where he wanted to go as fast as he wanted to get there.

Date Bait lobby card

Usually, where there was Gary, there was Steve. This was the case on the set of *Date Bait* (1960), another low budget teen flick in which Gary and a young lady named Marlo Ryan had the dubious honor of starring. Dale produced and directed it, which easily explained why Gary and Steve were in the cast. Gary again called this one "the worst movie ever made" although, in his opinion, "Steve was wonderful," even though his role was a small one. He said the same thing about *Dragstrip Riot* so clearly, Gary wasn't all too enamored of the plots on either of these movies. He was happy, however, with the end-result, the paycheck.

The crew and actors tended to know each other, and be friends, working together from one project to another. Nicholas Carras, also the musical lead on *Dragstrip Riot*, composed the music. *Date Bait* was most often double-billed at the drive-in with *High School Caesar*. This one held on in drive-ins for a few years, giving Gary and Marlo Ryan a limited place in the memories of teenagers around the country.

About this time, Steve was supplementing his income by working on construction crews. Even when he was away from the stage, acting was on his brain. One day during an especially long time in the hot sun, he looked forward to an evening in front of his television. He could be as much of a fan as anyone else who loved the medium and he had pegged this night as a special evening to watch Laurence Olivier, one of his favorite actors. Olivier would be on the tube at six PM, and Steve was determined to be home by then and settled into a comfortable viewing position.

Gary would be home before him, and he asked Gary to turn on the set and tune it to the right channel so he could just come in and plant himself in his favorite chair, and be ready. They lived in an upstairs apartment of a house. Steve rushed up the stars, threw off his jacket and haphazardly dropped his lunch pail on the kitchen counter. Like the good and loyal friend he was, Gary turned on the TV as Steve had asked of him.

"We used to have hot tea and honey toast in the evenings," Gary explained. Steve was completely oblivious to anything but the screen in front of him as Gary took the honey out of the refrigerator to prepare their snack. Forever the jokester, he couldn't resist simply dropping a lump of cold honey on Steve's toast with only a half-hearted effort at spreading it.

Then he kindly handed his friend his toast as Steve sat with his attention glued to the television. "Sipping hot tea, with three-quarter inches of cold, solid honey on toast," Gary explained, "the honey [eventually] started dripping on his hand. Steve absently licked at it but was unaware of what it was, or what he was doing..." until the gooey, sticky mess dripped all the way down his arm. As he watched him, Gary was reduced to an uncontrollable fit of giggles.

He remembered another time, and another mood which exhibited the spectrum and strength of their friendship. One day they went to breakfast at a restaurant on Sunset and LaBrea, a place they often frequented. Something was bothering Gary and he felt uncharacteristically antsy. Steve could tell he was on edge, and suggested they get out of the house awhile and he would help him talk it out. Their destination was packed that particular morning. As soon as they walked in the door, they immediately realized this might not be the best place for Gary in his current mood.

In fact, a stranger did try to pick a fight, for no particular reason except possibly Gary's contagious troubled mood, which was far too obvious. "I whirled on the guy with an angry expression," Gary admitted. "Steve stepped between us, and we got a table. He diffused the situation in a second. He did that sort of thing often." Between the two of them, Steve was usually the one who played the troublemaker on screen, yet he most often took on the real-life role of peacemaker. "Steve was like a

Pvt. Steve Ihnat, United States Army; photo compliments Ihnat Family Collection

dad," Gary remembered. "He was an old soul. It was as if he'd been around a long time. He was a protector."

* * *

As a recent news clipping had indicated, Steve considered becoming a United States citizen and even started the formal process without finalizing the effort. The idea may have precipitated or been in conjunction with his entrance into the Army in late 1960, in which he served for two years at Headquarters United States Army, Port Inchon, South Korea. "I wound up… running the entire dock unloading operations… as a PFC."

His time in the service wasn't always physically easy on him. Steve had scoliosis, a condition he dealt with from birth. Sometimes it gave him no trouble at all, and at other times, it caused him a good deal of pain. The Army allowed him special dispensation and he was able to stand during classes and meetings if necessary. He was allowed to walk around or go to the back of the room as needed. His acceptance into the armed services with such physical limitations spoke to the needs of the country at that time in history. Steve was able-bodied otherwise, and his back issue didn't stop him from doing anything he wanted to do, or he felt was necessary for him to do. The scoliosis was most often more of an aggravation at that early stage in his life.

Steve wrote and did artwork. While he was in the Army, he used these talents as an outlet for his creativity when there was free time. During his first year as Private Ihnat, Steve won Second Prize in the Republic of Korea's poetry contest for his entry, "Toil in the Night." His poem arose from the work he did day in and day out.

"From wheelhouse window I stand and gaze
   At steel strung booms –
   suspended
   looms
       hovering
Over head insignificant –
       on decks below.
They push and tow –
     and pull
At cargo heavy –
      holds full
          bellies empty
              heads heavy
                  backs tired
                     hands gloveless
Cold.
While home by fire sit wife and child
       awaiting day
When home will bring –
         some fish
           some bread
             some rice.
Perhaps –
      some welcome unpriced laugh.
That weary man becomes a King.
A tugboat shrieks –
     winch strained
       growls
         wind howls
Night holds us –
      one.
Then day breaks
         to
            night's torments tame.
I look again –
            eyes different –
              hearts same.

His Army stint was an experience he didn't ask for but one he grew to appreciate. He proved to be an expert in using a rifle, and he brought home a Good Conduct medal. The time away from Los Angeles ultimately stalled his determination to build his name in the acting world, which greatly disappointed and frustrated him.

Once he was discharged and returned to the States, he was forced to play a frantic game of professional catch-up. The industry had changed in the two years he was out of circulation. He and Gary remained in close contact through letters and when he got back to town, they hooked up again, and found another apartment together.

For the next few years, Steve picked up roles here and there, and he took whatever came his way. One part, in particular, was meaty and gave him a chance to really sink his teeth into a well-recognized story. Though his part wasn't large, he jumped at the chance to be in the cast of *Sweet Bird of Youth* when it was put on at the Civic Playhouse in Los Angeles in late 1961. Others in the cast were Jeremy Slate, then well-known to television viewers, and the lead female, Helena Nash, who had a moderately successful TV career. Steve was in good company for one of his first forays into professional stage work.

He continued on his designated path, pulling in a handful of bit parts on episodic television in 1961. There was an unnamed role in *Ripcord*, and another in *Target: The Corruptors*. There was also a part in *Day In Court*. This was another opportunity for Steve to hone his growing improvisational skills. He was able to take the gist of a scene, rapidly digest it, and run with it in his own words and actions. His acting style worked well when the action was only loosely scripted and actors were expected to be able to accurately portray the story and emotions behind it to the audience.

America had developed a fascination with what went on inside the courtroom, and *Day In Court* was one of the early television shows to give the viewing public a look at the justice system in action, long before *Court TV* or *The People's Court*. The show was as realistic as it could be, looking at how trials were conducted. Re-enactments of actual cases were played, and real attorneys made their arguments in front of real judges. The only actors were those used in place of the defendants and witnesses.

It was the fall of 1962, and he and Gary still regularly ran around with beautiful blonde actress, Connie Stevens. She was playful and perky, and a bit of a tease. She seriously dated Gary, and not-so-seriously dated Steve. She and Steve even wrote together, coming up with a TV script for *Hawaiian Eye*, titled, "The Diamond Head Dead," which they managed to sell to Warner TV. Connie was the female lead for the show, playing Cricket Blake opposite Robert Conrad who was Tom Lopaka. Their script, unfortunately, never made it into production.

Gary recognized Steve's stellar acting ability even that early in their association. He spoke of a memory he associated with an episode of *The Virginian* about a year or so after he became a regular on the show. Brian Keith was the main guest star. Steve would often stop by the set to see Gary and he became well-known as a regular visitor. James Drury, who starred as The Virginian, with no other name ever used, remembered Steve and Gary "were always having a hilarious time together... a lot of humor in their relationship. Always telling each other jokes... a lot of laughter between the two of them."

Mr. Drury felt Steve's years growing up and working on his family farm put him in good form for all the Westerns which came his way during his career. "I was impressed immediately when I saw him get on a horse because he obviously knew what he was doing," he said. "I really admired the guy and got along well with him."

During this particular visit of Steve's to the set, when Steve had yet to guest star on the show, Brian Keith was going through the script and running his lines, having difficulty with his part. Gary remembered Steve was watching Brian. He offered a few suggestions, which were gratefully accepted. Steve told Brian he "needed guts" in the role, and Steve ran the part for Brian as he would do it, not only reading the lines but getting into the physical action, grabbing dirt from beneath his feet and carrying out the emotion of the scene. Gary said Steve was intuitive as to what would work for such a character. Brian Keith was happy with Steve's input.

There was also more work on the stage in those days. From Mid-April to Mid-August of 1963, Steve starred at the Sherman Oaks Playhouse in *Fourposter* with a young, as-yet undiscovered Jeannine Riley, only a few months before *Petticoat Junction* appeared on TV to bring her a starring vehicle of her own. This play was the story of a married couple and their troubles and triumphs. They worked Thursday through Sunday evenings, just one of many versions of this play going on in various cities in California. This would've been one of the first opportunities in California for Steve to see his name listed as a lead actor in production credits.

In October, he was given a role as Doctor Matthews in an episode of *Bob Hope Presents The Chrysler Theatre*. "Something About Lee Wiley" garnered two Emmy award nominations, one for Outstanding Writing

Achievement in Drama and another in Outstanding Directorial Achieve-ment. The story chronicled certain events in the life of a historical real-life jazz singer popular in the 1930s. While still in her teens, before her career started, Lee Wiley fell from a horse and suffered a bout of blindness due to the accident.

Steve played her optometrist. Though his role wasn't big and came early in the production, he made an impression even before the show aired. There was a big screen movie being formulated and executives were watching him. Though he didn't know it then, Steve made such an impact with his work as Doctor Matthews he was pegged for a role, albeit a small one, in a Sam Spiegel creation, a movie ultimately to be called *The Chase*. This was two years before the casting efforts were ongoing but ideas were circulating, and Steve Ihnat was already on their radar as a result of this one television role.

* * *

As a regular on the show, Gary Clarke helped Steve get an audition for what would become his first of four guest roles on *The Virginian*. Steve read for, and got the part of, Stub O'Dell in an episode titled "The Fatal Journey." Steve played one of a band of outlaws who caused The Virginian extreme grief in a search for his girlfriend.

James Drury, who made the title character famous, discussed in an in-terview what he remembered most about Steve. "We were quite impressed with him. He had the quality of a chameleon. Changed from one character to another without any trouble at all. He could play any character at all without any question." This episode came out in early December 1963.

Steve worked steadily, most often cast as the villain, and quickly got to a point where he was finding jobs in almost any and every episodic TV show on the air. In the last month of the year, with his dark, striking looks, and his acting chops growing stronger every day, the chances to portray the darker side of humanity were beginning to cement the sort of charac-ter the viewing public wanted to see out of him. Or, at the very least, the sort of roles the casting directors wanted to send his way.

That same month, Steve took on the role of a bully rancher, Ben Wade, in an episode of *Temple Houston* titled, "Seventy Times Seven." The story told of a family of pacifist homesteaders who found themselves up against a group of aggressive cattlemen, headed by Steve's character. Jef-frey Hunter was the star, and Jack Elam played the Marshal, putting Steve in good, experienced company. He held his own with both of them, and then some.

That year proved to be one of great professional growth for Steve. He began getting more and more work, with his phone continually ringing to send him on auditions, most of which he won. Though he couldn't call any one role as a standout, he was gaining growing visibility, and he took it any way he could get it.

Steve and Gary's friendship stayed strong, working on their own as the jobs came to them and, when they had the chance, they would work as a pair. They lived together, and they partied together. Gary told of a spot they frequented, the Peppermint West, which was opened on North Cahuenga Boulevard by a New York fashion designer who called herself Marusia. She also owned the Peppermint Lounge on the East Coast.

When the twist became the latest dance craze and Marusia one of its biggest fans, she decided to dedicate a club to the fad in Los Angeles. The result was the West Coast counterpart, one of the newest places for the trendiest stars and up-and-coming ingénues to be seen. The likes of Zsa Gabor, Kim Novak, Janet Leigh, Troy Donahue, Jayne Mansfield, George Hamilton, Ann-Margret, and Tab Hunter, among many others, were known to twist the night away at the Peppermint West.

Gary and Steve became regulars. According to Gary, the club had "good food and a raised stage, good music groups, a dance floor" and, of course, "lovely girls." He told of one night when they found themselves socializing with two of those lovely young ladies. The four of them left the club and they went to the apartment in the house Gary and Steve rented. As the charming young men they knew they were, the guys showed the girls around their small and sparse home, with their focus going almost immediately to the bedrooms. One was larger than the other, and it held a queen-sized bed and very little else. The other had only a twin bed. The rest of the place consisted of a living room, a bathroom, and a kitchen.

Once the ladies finished the tour and they were settled into the living room, Gary and Steve fixed drinks. While in the kitchen alone, with only one focus on their minds, they did a coin toss for the big bedroom. There was no doubt in what direction this evening was headed, and neither of them wanted anything to mess up their plan. Gary won the toss, and he left the kitchen grinning.

The plan moved forward, going off heavenly without a hitch. It was obvious the ladies had the same intentions as Gary and Steve when they came home with them. In short order, the lights were off, the scene was set with music, and the couples were separating to move off into their respective bedrooms. For a little while, all was well. Everyone was busy.

Suddenly, Gary and his lady friend were interrupted by a loud crash and a high-pitched scream. They looked at each other, and Gary threw a blanket around himself, running to the other room. Steve's girl somehow managed to roll herself backward over the other side of the twin bed and crash flat onto the floor. When everyone knew she was okay, the humor in the situation bubbled up and they all were laughing hysterically. Needless to say, however, the original mood was ruined for all of them.

* * *

Screen jobs of no substance, just filler parts, plugged in the holes between meatier roles. Steve wasn't yet being offered "star" guest roles, yet he was noticed often enough to get really good and visible work on a regular basis. The paychecks kept coming and with every new gig, his face became a bit more familiar, both to audiences and, even more important now, to casting directors.

In the spring of 1964, Steve was allowed to expand his skills and his character repertoire with the part of Professor Roy Lucas, a young college science teacher at odds with an older, much more experienced professor in "Christmas Day is Breaking Wan," from *Channing*, a show which starred experience actor, Henry Jones. The episode's title was taken from "Christmas In India," a Rudyard Kipling poem, and this role was based more on an emotional struggle than the rough-and-tumble parts Steve usually took on.

This role appeared to have been Steve's first story-driven character, taking him away from the storylines where he was required to react to action rather than emotion. *Channing*, originally titled *The Young and the Bold* and with a plot which centered on Channing College staff and students, didn't last long and was ultimately cancelled mid-season. It served its purpose, however, in Steve Ihnat's career.

Chapter Three

ONE MAGAZINE ARTICLE WROTE OF STEVE, "He can't be called an overnight sensation because he knocked about Hollywood for years, starving, working at odd jobs, trying to push open studio gates. He got his first break on TV's *The Outer Limits* and after that he was in demand." That role in 1964 as Lieutenant Mims in a two-part segment titled, "The Inheritors," became an iconic part for him. Surprisingly, considering the trajectory his career was on of late, this wasn't a traditionally dark character. He could have never known what impact Lieutenant Mims would have on the future of his career.

The story centered around four American soldiers, rather average soldiers, all of them. That is, until each, in separate instances, including Steve's Lieutenant Mims, were shot in the head during battle. Each one was mysteriously shot by bullets made from fragments of a meteorite. By all accounts, these men should have died. The story, outlandish if a part of any other type of show besides one such as *The Outer Limits*, had each man disappearing from everyday society only to later appear with their brains developed far above the average human brain. The men had no idea what happened when they found themselves following an agenda they were incapable of denying, with an outcome they couldn't anticipate and wouldn't understand if they could.

His mind implanted with ominous instructions from an unseen otherworldly figure, Mims spearheaded what proved to be an enigmatic effort to take sad, seemingly unwanted children to another planet. The character of Lieutenant Mims was written to appear to be an evil sort throughout the entire story. Yet Steve played this man in such a desperately human way that viewers couldn't possibly know what was going on in his mind, or what he would do next. It wasn't until the very end when the truth came out and when it did, the tale proved to be an all-out character-driven storyline with a completely unexpected finale.

There were a number of child actors with whom Steve worked throughout the two-part show. One was Suzanne Cupito, a beautiful thirteen year old girl who went on to become Morgan Brittany, an even more beautiful adult actress with an extensive acting resume, best-known for her part in *Dallas*, the well-known TV show which ran from 1981 – 1987. She took the *Dallas* ride from the beginning to the end of the series. Her work in television, theater, and film began in 1960 when she was only nine years old and has never really ended. She has since become a political pundit on television and the internet.

Ms. Brittany found Steve Ihnat to be "a very intense actor.... Working with a child, many of the adult actors didn't have a very good rapport with children. In fact, a lot of them just dismissed you. But he was very giving as an actor. When we ran rehearsal and did dialogue, he sat right beside the bed. I had to be reading Braille in a book. He had his hand on top of my hand and he was very intense. What that did, that made me more intense for my performance. That was really great, especially for a young actor. A lot of times, kids are kind of an afterthought. They're great but [other adults think], 'I have to get into my thing.' He was busy giving."

She went on to compare Steve to one of the most celebrated and well-known actors in the history of Hollywood. "There were a few actors in my career who were like that. Henry Fonda was one of them. Steve reminded me a lot of Henry Fonda. He really did. They were very quiet on set. Very to themselves. Very into what they were doing that day. And very prepared. He was very, very similar to Henry Fonda."

During the second half of Part Two, Steve's character, Lieutenant Mims, collected the youngsters one-by-one to take them to the secret hideout. Each one expectantly waited for him though they really did not know why he was coming to whisk them away, or where they were going. Even he was clueless. He didn't know why he was tasked to take them from their current environments but he knew he was compelled to do so, with no power to do otherwise. When he retrieved Minerva, Morgan's blind character, his interactions with her were gentle and sweet.

Minerva was in a hospital room, sitting on the bed when he entered. She was dressed but not wearing shoes. She immediately called him by name, though she couldn't see him and they had never met. They were completely comfortable with each other. He told her to get ready to leave immediately, and then he picked up one of her shoes in one hand. With the other, he took her foot and lightly placed it on his thigh as he stood beside her bed. All the while, he talked to her in soothing tones, and she smiled in the direction of his voice.

In an interview, Morgan was asked if Steve's actions—the way he took hold of her foot to tie her shoe in a very intimate, fatherly sort of way to get her shoes put on quickly—was part of the plan. She said it had not been in the script. "That was something he did. He did it on his own. That was not directed. It was something that came out of how he felt. It was great for me. I couldn't react. I couldn't look at it [because she was supposed to be blind] but I could feel it. It was all him."

The day they filmed the scene where Lieutenant Mims took the kids away in the car to their unknown future was an excruciatingly hot one in Los Angeles. Morgan sat in the back seat as Steve started the car. The script called for her to lean over the front seat toward him, saying she "wants to see" what he looked like, in the way a blind person would "see" someone, with her hands.

As she touched his face, she was crying. Steve also produced tears, one which ran down his cheek. Very endearing, and all part of the script. What wasn't part of the script, however, was the heavy perspiration he could not control. The scene had to be done again and again because each time she put her fingers to his face to "see" him, and then moved away from him, she was covered in face paint.

"We actually started laughing because when I would put my hand on his face, his make-up would come off," Morgan explained, giggling at the memory. "It was so hot we were just dying. We couldn't wait to get that scene over so we could get out of that car." Amid the repeated makeup touch-ups and scene do-overs, they eventually managed to get a deeply touching final take. Both remained thoroughly professional and pleasant for the rest of the afternoon. Not a single viewer would have ever known of the difficulties involved in getting the scene completed.

Steve had a monologue at the end of the second part, all of which was carefully written for his character. He read through

Steve with Morgan Brittany in tear-filled scene from *The Outer Limits*, "The Inheritors"

what he was expected to say. He soaked it all in, and then respectfully asked Jim Goldstone, the director, if, instead, he could do the scene ad lib. He wanted to utilize the same intent and emotion but do so in his own way. Goldstone, who ultimately became a good friend, gave him the go-ahead.

Steve took a bit of time to immerse himself in the lieutenant's life at that moment, the emotions he believed the man would have felt in the situation he was in. Then Steve, the actor, spoke the words he, as Lieutenant Mims, was compelled to say. Steve's own words were literally so powerfully delivered that another actor, and many viewers, declared Steve Ihnat should have won an Emmy for his work.

His monologue, completely without any written forethought except for the script, which he used only as an outline, has over the years since become the centerpiece of the entire two-part episode of "The Inheritors" and has helped make it an episode which has never been forgotten.

Morgan Brittany said, "He put it into his own words. He put it into the way he felt it should be. Not a word-for-word memorization. It just came out so beautifully. To me, it made the whole show. It just touched me so much." She added, "The day we did the sequence with the spaceship, when we were on the soundstage and he did his monologue, you've never in your life seen crew members so mesmerized. Just silence on the set. It was amazing, an amazing performance. We all saw it." That scene became one of the signature roles of Steve Ihnat's entire career.

Morgan offered entertaining anecdotes about snafus which happened during taping. "About the rocket ship and the door… we were working some long hours on that day. When the front door had to be lowered and come down, and the kids had to walk up inside, it wouldn't work right. They tried to get it to smoothly come down but it would jerk all the way. The poor prop guys tried to do everything they could to get it work."

Steve with the children at the end of *The Outer Limits*, "The Inheritors"

She laughed delightedly at the memory. "And then they had an issue with Robert Duvall and the force field. They made a piece of glass in a wooden frame [as the force field]. He had to go stand right up against it but he kept breathing and his breath would keep coming up on the glass." The scene had to be re-shot and, she finished, they "had an interesting day that day." She explained that for each hour of the show, it took about seven days to film.

One reviewer declared that though Robert Duvall was excellent in *The Outer Limits'* "The Inheritors," his vote for Best Actor of the entire season would go to Steve Ihnat. "As the mysterious Lieutenant Minns, Ihnat is both menacing and tortured. In fact, right up to the climax we're not sure if he's here to save Earth or destroy it. He's one of those rare actors who can say lines of dialogue with his eyes." Another wrote, "… he was such an iconoclastic presence as a guest star throughout every TV series in the sixties." One male reviewer stated point-blank, "… it's Ihnat's show all the way, and he sells it throughout with those big soulful eyes."

Unbeknownst to Steve, one evening as *The Outer Limits* episode in which he appeared aired on television, his future was watching him. A beautiful young woman was in her living room in front of the TV with her husband. Steve caught her eye, and even though she sat there with the man to whom she was married, she could not hide how enthralled she was with the enigmatic man playing Lieutenant Mims. Her husband asked, "You really like him, don't you?" The woman, named Sally, could only reply, "He's a brilliant actor!"

Little did she know at the time how her life, and Steve Ihnat's life, would eventually intersect.

But Steve Ihnat didn't yet know Sally Carter. He was only beginning to cement relationships to carry him through to the end of his life in ways he could not even begin to imagine. In the fall, Steve was seen in an episode of *Slattery's People.* The show was titled, "Remember the Dark Sins of Youth?"

One of the other guest stars was Ed Asner. Steve crossed paths with Ed a few months earlier that year, 1964, when they were both seen on *Bob Hope Presents the Chrysler Theatre's,* "A Case of Armed Robbery." They'd had little contact with each other but Ed had greatly impressed Steve. He had no way of understanding right then what Ed would come to mean to him.

*　*　*

One movie experience which never made a public splash but which was enjoyed by Steve and his co-star, Gary Clarke, was in a second-rate

Sally Carter, the future Mrs. Steve Ihnat; photo compliments
Ihnat Family Collection

"adult-themed" storyline titled *Passion Street U.S.A.* (1964) It also had two other titles. *Bourbon Street U.S.A.* was used in some promotional materials, and *Hot Rain* made it into a few listings, though it never stuck. Gary played an Episcopalian minister who fell in love with, and married, a hooker. At the same time, she was having an affair. The hooker was played by a pretty young actress named Tanya Conway who, away from the cameras, was in reality Steve's girlfriend. Steve, working under the name of Steve Quinn for this production, played Dick Budman, a jealous detective.

The movie was shot entirely on location in New Orleans. Tanya's character

Passion Street U.S.A., aka *Bourbon Street, U.S.A.* newspaper ad... adults only

was a confused young girl who left her family and moved to the French Quarter to make it on her own. Lost, finding herself in the wrong circles and lonely in her new environment, she met and fell in love with a kindly minister, played by Gary. With the two of them, as usual, in character, Gary as the savior in white and Steve as the evil one in darkness, Steve

Steve as the bad boy with Tanya Conway in *Passion Street U.S.A.*

wanted the girl for himself and didn't care what he did to get her. He pulled every dirty trick he could think of to kill her chaste romance with the man of God.

Unfortunately for the minister, his hooker-wife couldn't resist Steve's sexy character and dark good looks, and she began an affair with him while remaining married to her holy husband. When the minister discovered her duplicity, as Gary related the story, "he visited a local pub, got drunk, sang 'St. James Infirmary,' climbed the 20-foot statue of Andrew Jackson on horseback—in Jackson Square across the street from Cafe Du Monde—and ripped off his collar, denouncing God." He then climbed down from the statue and, Gary finished, "had coffee and a beignet." Gary's sense of humor in current-day indicated how silly he considered the entire script.

Passion Street U.S.A. played in late 1964 in drive-ins, double-billed with other "adult" films for late night crowds going to the movies. Most of those audiences weren't there for just the story on the big screen in front of them. This one was considered risqué for the time. Gary and Steve, it

Gary Clarke as the wronged minister, with Tanya Conway in *Passion Street U.S.A.*

seemed, took the roles as much for the fun of going to New Orleans as they did for any potential artistic reasons which could possibly have been considered.

Gary animatedly related one of their escapades while they were in the Big Easy. "I was in my minister's wardrobe, collar and all, mid-day, walking along Basin Street with Steve. We were on a break. We came upon a pushcart ice cream vendor stopped by the curb. The day was warm and I asked Steve if he would like to indulge. He reached for money and I said, 'This is on me.'"

Gary went up the vendor and told him what he wanted, about to pay for the ice cream, when the man told him, "Oh, no, Father, you have sacrificed enough. This is the least I can do."

Gary replied in his best Fatherly-type voice, "Thank you, my son, but I cannot ask you to pay for my wayward son here beside me."

"Please, Father," the vendor replied. "Perhaps it may lead him to seeing the error of his ways."

Gary, without stepping out of character, no smile, didn't skip a beat. Steve just stood beside him, and remained mute and repentant. "Thank you, my son," Gary said to Mr. Ice Cream Man. "May God bless you."

Gary and Steve strolled away with their ice cream, the vendor none the wiser.

Another experience had the two men at dinner after work one evening. They were housed in a top-floor apartment of the Court of Two Sisters in the French Quarter. They were friends with some of the waiters in the restaurant and would go out on the town with them. One of these nights, a girl slyly came to their table while they were enjoying their meal. She seemed to take an obvious liking to Steve, and without invitation, sat with them. She chatted him up, listening to the music with them, and then ordered champagne. At some point Steve was distracted, and the girl disappeared, leaving him with only an empty bottle and the bill for fifty bucks.

Steve didn't have that kind of money. Neither did Gary. Steve found himself in a heated discussion with the restaurant manager who expected to have the champagne bill paid. He wasn't interested in Steve's hard-luck tale. Finally one of Steve's cast members showed up and helped him out.

This proved to be one of those sort of films an actor working his way up the industry food chain probably hoped to have forgotten in short order. It continued to play for a number of years, however, thanks to drive-ins and the young men and women who frequented them for reasons other than the quality of the movie. *Passion Street* was the perfect backdrop for those teenaged activities. The film then disappeared into oblivion and seems to have been lost to time.

* * *

Steve continued to hone his craft every chance he got. October was a busy month for him on the small screen. He was seen in early October with Lloyd Bochner, Bobby Darin, and, in her first dramatic television role, movie actress Janet Leigh, in "Murder In The First" from *Bob Hope Presents the Chrysler Theatre*. Steve was able to be a good guy this time, as Lieutenant Malloy who investigated the murder of Ms. Leigh's character, Mrs. Carol Hartley. Mrs. Hartley had tried to break off an affair with Brad Kubec, played by Bobby Darin, a stuttering law student. Lloyd Bochner was her husband.

Three days later, Steve again showed up in living rooms around the country via the TV screen, in a role which may have been the precursor to what became a sort of signature role for him, that of the exotic, foreign, mysterious bad guy. On *Voyage to the Bottom of the Sea*, in an episode titled "The Price of Doom," he was a scientist named Pennell. He was used in the beginning and gone almost just as quickly, and though his part was quite small, his character was one of three guests on board the submarine suspected of being a foreign agent.

Someone, one of these men, intentionally carried dangerous samples of plankton aboard the Seaview. His wife was played by Pat Priest, who ultimately went on to become the only "normal" family member in the campy show, *The Munsters*. From this point on, Steve seemed destined to most often be seen as villain material.

Steve with Pat Priest in *Voyage to the Bottom of the Sea*; photo compliments Barbara Peterson

He soon after crossed paths with a man who would become a good friend and business partner. Steve Lodge had his first real job as a costumer on *The Fugitive*, an episode titled, "Cry Uncle," which aired in December. The press dubbed the story, "a melodramatic tearjerker only recommended for the softest of hearts." Steve's role was small and, as Steve Lodge said, he "got

Steve with Gene Roddenberry; photo compliments Ihnat Family Collection

to know him a little bit. No one introduces you. I just hung his costumes and told him which ones to wear in the scenes where he was supposed to be wearing them."

Steve was also making other connections in the industry with actors and writers who would prove to have careers long into the future. He carefully and intentionally laid the groundwork, becoming genuinely friendly with such men as Arthur Hill, Ed Asner, and Gene Roddenberry, among others. These people would ultimately act with him and for him, or write material in which he would act. They got along well, and understood each other.

* * *

Early the next year, Steve was seen in "Robert A. Taft," an episode of *Profiles In Courage*. The show was a lofty effort at historical truth offered to the masses on television, telling stories of lesser-known people who stood their ground during difficult situations. The show was based on President John F. Kennedy's Pulitzer Prize-winning book and lasted for twenty-six episodes, with each one featuring a figure from American history who took a societally-unpopular stand during a critical period.

Seven of eight senators from Kennedy's book were profiled, with the episode in which Steve appeared focusing on Illinois Republican Senator, Robert A. Taft. Taft questioned the legality of the Nuremburg trials and in doing so, lost him his party's presidential nomination, even endangering the party in the process. Actor Lee Tracy played the Senator, and Steve played the part of Tom Smith, best known in historical circles related to Taft when Smith engaged him in a series of radio debates published as *Foundations of Democracy* (1930).

Reportedly, President Kennedy personally approved all details of the show, including the actors, directors, and others involved. The first thirteen episodes of the series were filmed before the show went on the air so this may have really been a very early credit in Steve's career.

* * *

From then on, Steve Ihnat worked constantly, and 1965 could informally be considered the year his star took solid root in the industry. Even if his wasn't a high profile star, his phone was now always ringing and there was always a new job awaiting him. It wasn't long before he was steadily making between $60,000 and $70,000 a year as a character actor, a comfortable place to be in the unstable world of Hollywood make-believe.

Yet still, Steve was not satisfied. He would not be satisfied until he moved up to the next level, and then to the next. He knew he was destined for even more, and he could not stop, he would never stop, reaching. More. It wasn't in his nature to simply stay comfortable.

In the spring of 1965, Steve was once again cast as an antagonist, if only as a drunken reprobate named Kaster. Critics said, "The show is handled so matter of factly, the plot is almost believable." Steve was an enlisted soldier who double-crossed Major Cantwell, a retiring commanding officer of an Army outpost, in "Retreat," from *Rawhide*. Cantwell was demoted because of a record-keeping infraction of which he was inno-

Steve with Eric Fleming in *Rawhide*

cent. In anger, he stole $30,000 in Army cash the day before he left the service. He put the cash in a package addressed to himself, to be mailed out at the nearest town.

Kaster, previously severely punished by Cantwell for drinking on duty, left the Army and joined a trail drive. He stole Cantwell's package, hoping to find liquor in it. A hot and heavy pursuit ensued. A reviewer said Steve put in "one of his usual quirky, intriguing turns here."

He had another movie role in the spring, if only a brief one, and one in which he wasn't even officially credited in promotional material. *Brainstorm* (1965) was reviewed as "a suspenseful, well-acted film." Steve played Dr. Copeland, an intern at a mental institution where star, Jeff Hunter, was sent while feigning insanity after murdering the husband of his paramour, a "nympho-alcoholic," played by Anne Francis. Produced by William Conrad, the picture was filmed in part at the Veterans Administration Hospital on Wilshire Boulevard in Los Angeles. If nothing else, Steve found himself keeping good company with solid acting talent, and received a paycheck in the bargain.

In June, he received notice when *The Chase* (1966) starring Marlon Brando, started ramping up, the film he was pegged for a few years earlier. He was signed to the cast by famed director Sam Spiegel, who put out such celebrated films as *The Bridge on the River Kwai* (1957) and *On The Waterfront* (1954), and notifications started filtering out to the press.

"Clifton James and Steve Ihnat have joined the cast as two town toughs who menace Marlon Brando...." The leads were the heavy-hitting stars of the time—as well as Brando, there was Robert Redford, Jane Fonda, E.G. Marshall, Angie Dickinson, and quite a few others. Though Steve's role wasn't a lead, it was crucial to the story. Casting him among a line-up of solid movie actors showed a vote of confidence in his talent.

In the original script, Archie Cloud had dialogue. Yet in the final version, Archie remained silent the entire time he was on screen. The reason for this, according to Sally, came as the result of a direct request from Steve himself. Few actors would give up a chance to have dialogue but, contrary to the norm, Steve didn't usually take the predictable approach. In Archie Cloud, he saw something unique, and he felt the character would come off as much stronger if he played him in a totally unexpected way. Archie would not speak.

After studying the script from beginning to end, he felt he could better play up Archie's gloominess if he didn't say a word. He was sure Archie would prove to be more frightening and threatening if he delivered him to the viewing audience this way. Steve knew there was more potential in

Steve with Marlon Brando in *The Chase* before the fight scene was shot;
photo compliments Ihnat Family collection

Archie's personality within the emotion of the storyline without having any words spoken. In turn, this would strengthen the entire movie.

The director allowed him to run with it. Doing so, Steve shorted himself a speaking role, yet he made Archie, and himself, more visible in the final product. The result proved to be a more menacing Archie Cloud, causing the character to be memorable for years to come. One unnamed Canadian newspaper reporter said Archie was one of "a trio of rednecks..." and Steve "...has a quietly sinister role to play but builds it up to the climax of the movie in which he figures predominantly."

Steve's part may have not been that big but it was hugely haunting. There was a vicious fight scene at the end with Brando, bloody and ugly on both ends. Archie Cloud ultimately had the final say on the overall reason for the story. That the man who enacted him held his own with Marlon Brando, and then some, was itself a credit to Steve's acting ability.

No matter the role or how big or small it was, Steve Ihnat became fully engrossed in his character. He was a consummate professional who took his work to heart and brought his characters fully to life.

* * *

The following year, Steve had a variety of roles to play. February of 1966 saw him as a drifter, in a *Gunsmoke* episode of the sort he had often been seen in already. "My Father's Guitar" was something of a soft, sentimental story. Only twenty five years old, Beau Bridges played a young man overly attached to his daddy's guitar, of great importance to him since his father died. After he killed a man who wanted to damage the guitar, he began to bury him. When he saw two riders coming his way, he rushed off toward Dodge.

Steve played Jack, one of those drifting riders. His only purpose that day was to go into Dodge for some drinking and carousing. He and his buddy got involved with the young guitar-toting, man-killer and, of course, Matt Dillon went after them. Steve was good at such parts, proving himself to be quite believable. He strode right into the role, seemingly effortlessly walking the walk, putting on just enough of a drawl, giving the impression he knew what it was like back then to live in those dusty, drunken, lawless Western days.

He stayed in the historical west of the United States that month, next seen in *The Big Valley* as a henchman to Sam Beldon, played by Harold Stone, a bad guy who kidnapped Victoria Barkley. Instead of meaning her any harm, however, Beldon wanted Victoria to teach him to read and write, an odd request from a known criminal. "Teacher of Outlaws" received good marks for its tender story related to the short-lived relationship between the Barkley matriarch and her pupil.

Steve had a good amount of screen time with acting great, Barbara Stanwyck. His role required him to help her in and out of a buggy, as well as get physically close to her and talk and stare into her eyes. His character, Will Hanley, brazenly flirted with her in a way which almost made the viewer's skin crawl. He never got his chance to make a move, though, because his boss was already sweet on her. By the time the episode neared the end, there were only three characters from the active story left standing—Victoria Barkley, Beldon, and Will—and, as was usually the case, Will, Steve's character, didn't get out alive.

In May, his role-playing went from a lecherous drunken bandit in the North American Old West to World War II Germany and double agents involved in espionage. In *Blue Light*, Steve took on the part of a Nazi general, a role he seemed to wear well. His family's Eastern European roots may have had something to do with this. Their departure from Czechoslovakia as the War swept into the area to change their way of life forever could have crossed Steve's mind as he prepared to step into the shoes of German Field Marshall Gerhardt in "Field of Dishonor."

Gerhardt denounced the Third Reich and all it stood for. The Germans, believing he was working for them, sent the show's star, David March, played by Robert Goulet, to find him and bring him to justice, German style. Yet March was a double agent, working against the Germans for the United States. March was forced to decide if Gerhardt was genuinely interested in defecting, or if he was playing him to find out if he was a traitor. If he believed Gerhardt to be on the up-and-up, March was to smuggle him out of the country. A review of the episode read it was "suspenseful, and too short."

Blue Light lasted only one season for seventeen episodes. Though the show received high marks during its time on the air for its acting and writing, the premise behind it was a lofty one, and quite possibly took on more of the growing international political atmosphere than television of the time was yet ready to handle. The year was 1966, and the Cold War was nearly at its apex. While *Blue Light*'s story concerned itself with World War II, the present time and circumstances were a direct result of what happened those twenty-some years earlier, and the atmosphere remained agitated.

Each episode was meant to tell a story about David March, as a double agent who operated behind enemy lines inside the Third Reich. March was not modeled after a real-life individual but series executive producer-director, Walter Grauman, explained, "While *Blue Light* is largely fictional, there is no reason to doubt that

Steve in *Blue Light*

such a man as its chief character did truly exist and operate during World War II." He continued, "...through it, there is a tremendous ring of truth. We are following closely many of the events of the war."

To enhance a sense of truth and realism, Grauman and his staff chose to film a great deal of the series in Germany. Easily recreated inside sets were done in Hollywood but where the actual backgrounds of historical events occurred, he wanted that to ring true, to show the "atmosphere of the Old World, which hasn't changed in centuries, and which existed during World War II...." He moved the entire production company to Munich, not an inexpensive endeavor.

Another tactic employed was the use of actors who were not American-born. The casting directors scoured "Germany and some of the surrounding countries for actors and actresses native to the territory." Grauman wanted audiences to know American TV viewers would see "a parade of Europe's finest actors and actresses... for realism and authenticity...."

Though he was by this time well-cemented in his North American lifestyle with no plans to ever again take up permanent residence in Europe, Steve Ihnat still suited Grauman's qualifications in every possible way. Just walking onto the set, Steve looked the part. Adding the right clothes, hairstyle, and makeup, he easily put on the perfect accent and inflections to become the double-dealing spy who attempted to out-spy the star of the show. This role fit him like a custom-made suit of clothes.

* * *

What the viewing public saw as a final product on TV was often no-where near the originally-pitched project, or what was even started after a contract was signed. Such was the case with a show ultimately called, *Iron Horse*. This was originally a two-hour movie titled, *Scalplock*, meant to be an ABC Sunday night feature. This did, in fact, show once as a Sunday night movie, and then again as a Wednesday evening offering, both earlier in the year.

It made no real splash in that format and so was revised into an hour-long version, inaugurating *Iron Horse* as a new TV show. Since this was now expected to become an ongoing series, additional episodes were needed. The first of the series was based on the original movie, and its title, initially, was "Rail Runs West." For whatever reason, this didn't suit the bigwigs. Another adaptation with rearrangement, and the final, final product became known as, "Joy Unconfined."(1966)

This preparation turned out good for Steve. He was hired as the lead guest star in the role of Luke Joy. The show starred Dale Robertson as Ben Calhoun and in this episode, Ben had won a railroad in a poker game. This posed a problem. His former partner, Luke Joy, wasn't happy because he claimed the line as rightfully his. Once again, Steve's ability to effort-lessly step into and become an angry Western character was put into play, and well-utilized.

Mid-fall, Steve found himself in the only true comedy role of his en-tire career, and probably arguably the only mediocre performance he ever gave. Cast as Sergeant Ben Roberts in, "My Master, the Rainmaker," an ep-isode of *I Dream of Jeannie*, Steve was required to stretch his skills toward making people laugh, instead of making them cringe in fear. He put on a fair American southern accent although he overdid the stereotype of a

Steve in *I Dream of Jeannie* with
Larry Hagman

"southern boy" from Alabama, and played his role to the hilt. His performance was enjoyable but must not have impressed many comedy casting directors since he never again received offers in the genre.

Right on the heels of that single comedy effort, Steve re-turned to one the characteriza-tions he knew best. He found himself playing R.G. Posey in,

Steve in *Shane*

"The Bitter, the Lonely" (1966) from *Shane*. This was the television version of the 1953 movie classic of the same name. Whereas the title character in the film was played by Alan Ladd, the star of the TV show was David Carradine, and he and Steve ultimately became friends.

Steve's character, Posey, was a cowboy dropout, a drifter with almost no schooling. Due to incidents in his past, he felt a deep-seated hatred for sod-busting homesteaders. Philosophical Shane told him at one point, "You're a loser, Posey. Born and bred. You just go on fighting and hating and beating that thick head of yours against each new day until you die out just like that dinosaur." This was a good representation of the man Steve played.

Virtually penniless, he was nonetheless ready to conquer the world, especially the peaceful world in which Shane lived. His lack of education and money made him an easy mark for a local who decided the new guy in town was the perfect person he needed to do his dirty work. One reviewer wrote, "Expect another 'high noon' scene at a stopped-up dam before it's over."

Once more that month, Steve took on the role of another drifter, another man on a horse moving from one town to another, this time in Mexico, out to give Matt Dillon on *Gunsmoke* a hard time in, "The Mission." This was the third of six episodes he would do for *Gunsmoke*. He was one of those actors who could appear on the same show more than once, playing a different character in a different story every time, and he fit believably into the script with each role.

This was one of Steve's blessings, or curses, depending on whose opinion mattered at any given moment. He had one of those faces and physiques which blended right into the scene and was immediately convincing. He could be "any man," and always was. The casting directors of so many shows utilized him for this reason.

As well, he was an excellent actor, he was reliable, and he was sensitive to the needs and the roles of the other actors. That he could come back time and time again as someone else was his icing on the cake. Not a single viewer would question this because he stepped inside the skin of a new character with every new storyline, and TV consumers never seemed to notice. If they did, they didn't care. In fact, they always wanted more of him. And as a guest star, since he was so often killed off at the end of these shows, he *had* to return as someone else.

Chapter Four

IN 1967, STEVE MANAGED TO BE VIOLENTLY KILLED a few more times. This year proved to be a turning point, and a memorable one for his personal and professional life.

Things started out much the same as they had in recent years. Parts came his way, and he accepted them. February's offering featuring Steve Ihnat was, surprisingly, not a Western. *The Felony Squad* starred Howard Duff and Ben Alexander. In "Target!" Steve played Victor Durant, a gang leader, who wanted to keep the previous mob leader from testifying against him. This was a new twist for him on his usual heavy role. Steve's character was suspected of spearheading the abduction of the former mobster to keep him away from the grand jury.

Of course, Victor Durant, aka Steve, died before this was all over.

In March, he played John Farron, again on *Gunsmoke*. The episode was "Noose of Gold," and Farron, a married man, was wanted for murder. Even though Steve had acted in Hollywood for a decade by this time, this show was notable in his career because it marked his first onscreen kiss. His wife, Edna, was played by Jan Shepard, in Hollywood even longer than he had been. If Steve were aware of her kissing "record" with fellow actors in previous shows in that season, he might not have agreed to play opposite her. Jan already acted as a "widow woman" in ten straight episodic television shows, and Steve's character, sadly for him, did not break her streak.

Yes, he died again.

He did go on to greater things that month, roles in which, as a result of last minute plans, he was actually allowed to live. He had a meaty part on the big screen in the movie, *In Like Flint* (1967), as General Carter. Filmed on location in Jamaica, this was not a bad gig, and *TV Guide* called his character "an ambitious general" who wanted to "blackmail the world with... a nuclear bomb." One review said of Steve that he "hit it out

WANTED

JOHN FARRON

$9,200 REWARD

☛ DEAD OR ALIVE ☚

For the Crimes of **MURDER** and **ARMED ROBBERY**

NOTIFY NEAREST LAW AUTHORITIES.

Steve in "Noose of Gold" on *Gunsmoke*

of the ballpark with his excellent portrayal of the sneaky and cunning General Carter."

Another wrote that he came on "pretty strong." In the original script, his character was to have been bumped off half-way through the film. However, as an article indicated, "…the producer likes his acting so much, the part is being re-written to let Steve 'live' thru [sic] to the end."

Steve was aware he was moving up the notoriety ladder in Hollywood but it didn't feel as if he was really getting all that far, and certainly not as fast as his visualization had him doing so. The parts he received became increasingly more substantial. His growing prominence was directly proportionate with the vast amount of work he was putting out on both the small and large screens, and occasionally on the stage. Yet the roles that came his way were heavily typecast, nearly always leaning toward the dark, bad guy, and of late, the internationally evil sort.

Steve as General Carter in *In Like Flint*

World politics were adapting to the changes across the globe. Countries worked against each other not necessarily always on the battlefield with guns and cannons at the ready, but utilizing a quiet, subversive way of fighting, and the entertainment world shifted its fare to keep up with the times. Offerings slowly gave viewers more of what was believed to be what the enlightened public wanted, a reflection of the real world around them. Whereas Hollywood started out as a place of make-believe, it was evolving into a mirror of humanity's social conscience.

* * *

The parts Steve Ihnat played by the time 1967 really took root showed he was well on his way to finding his footing in an industry that wasn't kind to actors without the ability to weather the low times. A short press piece by an unknown writer, titled, "Fame" in big letters, gave a general outline of his progress. It was something of a fluff piece, the sort of thing found in a fan magazine. His latest and greatest credits were listed, his age, and place of birth. The story of his family's harrowing departure from Czechoslovakia into Canada was glossed over, and his stint with the Pasadena Playhouse after he got to Hollywood was mentioned. But it was what they said about him, not directly as an actor but as a man, which gave the most insight into how he was growing in the industry, despite his own disappointed personal image of his progress in Tinseltown.

"He's a cross between Bob Mitchum," the article read, "Lee Marvin and James Coburn and you've got to admit that's pretty good crossing. During the past few years he's been cast mainly as 'heavies,' but he has the kind of dynamic sex appeal that can also make him a top ranking leading man...."

This was a confusing and in some ways emotionally overwhelming period in Steve's career. He was recently offered, and had signed, a seven-year contract with 20th-Century Fox. His first film under their umbrella was *In Like Flint*. Despite the contract, Steve continued to pile on movie and television credits, though not all of them were signed with 20th Century Fox.

During this period, there were press photos of Steve placed in the television guide section of the newspapers with the caption, "BUSY." His name was the only identifier included, no longer utilizing qualifying titles such as "character actor" or even "guest star." His appearances with the times and television stations of his appearances for that date, most often more than one on any given evening, were included under his picture. Seemed Steve Ihnat was finally well-known enough to viewers amongst a parade of countless and, mostly, nameless, guest actors to warrant such direct promotion.

He had become a true "star" guest star.

Steve did five more studio movies during his career. The timing for all of them fit into that seven-year period of the 20th Century contract he signed yet none were done with 20th Century Fox. What became of the contract, or why it may have fallen through, or even if it did fall through or something else happened to circumvent its fulfilment, is yet another mystery in the life of Steve Ihnat.

Early April brought Steve's second of two appearances on *The Fugitive*. In "The Walls of Night," Kimble, played by star David Janssen, fell in love with Barbara Wells, a role taken on by Janice Rule. Steve worked with Janice in the movie, *Chase*. Barbara worked at the same trucking company in Portland, Oregon, at which Kimble had secured a job. She fell for him, too. The problem—he wasn't the only one with a secret.

Barbara was on a prison work release program, unwilling to tell Kimble why she could have lunch with him but when work was over for the day, she couldn't see him in the evenings. Another problem in her life showed up in the form of Art Meredith, a male visitor she received like clockwork each day. Steve played Meredith, Barbara's parole officer. His insistent presence would continually frustrate her hopes and plans. Finally, Kimble learned of Barbara's situation and they ran away.

But Meredith was on the case. He discovered their relationship and in doing so, stumbled on Kimble's true identity, setting a trap to save the day by bringing the pair back to Portland. One review called this "an out-and-out love story." Another review said it "should appeal to the women." Steve was, as usual, not the leading man and, again as usual, not given a chance to get the girl.

In the middle of that month, Steve took a somewhat secretive trip to Monaco. To the casual onlooker who might have seen him there, he would have seemed to be just another gambler, and a lucky one at that. He managed to rack up $14,000 in chips at the gaming tables. This was but a bonus, though.

The flight across the pond was an official business trip. He was summoned to Rome by Dino de Laurentiis to audition for a part in a high-budget film directed by Edward Dmytryk. At the time it was titled *Battle of Anzio* (1968), the story of eight survivors of a Ranger outfit virtually annihilated by the Germans. Steve was eyed for one of the five top supporting roles. Robert Mitchum was the lead, having already previously taken on a handful of battle films, putting his solid mark on this genre.

Columbia Pictures produced this one. Again, for reasons unknown, Steve did not appear in the film which ultimately debuted under the title of, simply, *Anzio*. From his credits and his known personal schedule, he had no known projects in the offing during the movie's production months. His trip to Rome came on the heels of his success with *In Like Flint*, which likely got him the visibility to be called to court by de Laurentiis.

It is known, however, that de Laurentiis was said to have hired another actor for the same film simply on the power of that actor's name and visibility in the industry at that time. According to Michael Druxman, then-publicist for Edward "Eddie" Dmytryk, *Anzio*'s director, Peter Falk arrived on the movie set only to discover his part was virtually non-existent. He was about to use the return-home ticket given to him when Eddie assured him there would be a decent role available to him in *Anzio*.

How this de Laurentiis quirk may have applied to Steve is totally suppositional but it might show that he wasn't the only actor whose participation in this movie could have ended up as questionable. He hadn't shared any information about his trip to Rome, or his audition with de Laurentiis, with anyone at home before he left, which his friends and family considered unusual.

There may have been any number of other reasons, as well, which circumvented his involvement in what might have completely changed the trajectory of his career, moving him into a full-time A-list movie actor. The answer will never be known.

* * *

Poster for *Anzio*, the film Steve was slated to do but didn't make the final cast

Also in April, Steve returned to his family home in Canada to take his sisters and parents to see *In Like Flint* at The Century Theatre on Mary Street in Hamilton. This theater, in operation since 1912 and desperately in need of a makeover, was redecorated that year. The family loved the movie and all the attention Steve received as a result.

He was interviewed by the local paper, *The Spectator*, and when he was asked what he thought about how he was now "making good money," and about the success coming his way, his response was classically Steve. He still didn't feel his stock was rising all that much. "How long can you go up to bat without hitting a home run?"

The summer rolled around and something happened in his life that unquestionably changed his world forever. A chance meeting with a beautiful woman had Steve reevaluating his free-wheeling single days. He happened to attend a play one evening at the Horseshoe Stage, a small independent theater in the Los Angeles area. He saw a tall, dark-haired, beautiful and strikingly-shapely woman across the room. She appeared to be bored and uncomfortable, trying to figure out how to tactfully get away from a guy determined to pick her up during a cocktail party held after the play.

The woman saw Steve coming toward her but she was not prepared for what he would say to her. He walked up, getting deeply close, inside her personal space, and intentionally touched her elbow. He thoroughly ignored the other man.

She turned and gave her full attention to this handsome new stranger, whose face was somehow familiar though she didn't think she knew him. His first words to her were, "Excuse me, I think I love you."

She parried back, without thinking, "That's the right thing to say to me."

He bluntly asked for her phone number. No chit chat. No preamble.

She didn't even pretend that she wanted any. "I've nothing to write on."

"I'll remember it." She could tell he knew the look on her face said she didn't believe him. "I will remember," he repeated.

She saw his surprise when she shrugged and spit out her number. The other man, long since forgotten, finally gave up in the face of his clearly-winning competition, and moved on. This dark-haired stranger, who of course turned out to be Steve Ihnat, true to his word, remembered her phone number and called her two days later. The woman turned out to be Sally Carter. She realized she had seen him on TV years before when he played on *The Outer Limits*. That was why he seemed so comfortable to her from the moment he walked up.

During that initial phone call, they arranged their first official date. Steve asked Sally if she would like to do dinner with him at The Valley Tail O' The Cock in Studio City. She told him she had an appointment at UCLA but she would meet him at the restaurant afterward. Sally did not have any appointment that night but she didn't want to appear too eager... even though she was truly very eager. She met him there, the date went well, and she was hooked. She said he seemed to reciprocate the feelings.

As they were leaving the restaurant, he asked her the equivalent of, "Would you like to come up to my place and look at my etchings?"

Sally scoffed at him and asked if he was really going to pull that line on her.

"Well," he replied, apparently trying to look innocent, "I really do have some."

"Thanks, but no thanks." Sally said it killed her to walk out of the restaurant and away from Steve that night, but she did. She just couldn't allow herself to be immediately available when she felt something possibly so special was at stake. She got herself home, and found her phone ringing not long afterward.

Steve was on the other end of the line. "I guess I should've made sure you got home safely."

"Yes, I believe you should have." She laughed, and asked if he would like to come over for dinner soon. He agreed, equally as coy. They made a date for a week later.

It was clear to Sally they were both attracted to each other. The connection was wildly physical but that wasn't the only thing pulling them together. There was so much more. She was afraid to have this be fluff, to turn out to be only physical. She didn't want him to think she saw this as something casual so she tread very carefully. He was obviously doing the same thing.

The truth was, though, she did find him overwhelmingly desirable and pacing herself was not an easy task.

Steve and Sally in earlier days

They had dinner at her place for their next date and, the following was at his. She learned he truly did have etchings. His own etchings. Steve Ihnat was not only an actor, he was quite an accomplished artist, and his drawings and paintings showed great talent. The man proved to be full of surprises, and Sally Carter fell fully under his spell.

*   *   *

Steve, with Gary Clarke, in *Police Story*, what would have been Steve's own TV series; photo compliments Ihnat Family collection

In the autumn, something came about which emphasized Steve's words from that recent spring interview he did in Canada when he ruefully asked the reporter, not expecting an answer, "How long can you go up to bat without hitting a home run?"

He won the starring role as Captain James Paige in a made-for-TV movie, co-starring his best friend, Gary Clarke, as his assistant. *Police Story* (1967) was a television pilot, meant to be a mid-season NBC replacement and a thirty minute weekly show. This was the very show that brought Steve and Gary back together as friends after an unfortunate separation in their friendship of a few years. It was to have been their big break, an opportunity for their own starring vehicle both of them had waited a long time for, and both deserved after putting in so many years in the industry.

A write-up explained this evening's premiere would be "a 'sneak preview' starring Steve Ihnat as a captain in what can best be described as a composite of almost every station house you've ever seen...." He was the "kindly captain."

There was something odd, though. Some television write-ups indicated this wasn't a new offering. One wrote that NBC whipped out "another old pilot film that failed...." For whatever reason, the pilot was never picked up, whether written and offered at an earlier date, or just out this season. Maybe it didn't work because Steve had played too nice of a guy. Steve Ihnat as the good guy wasn't what was expected of him.

Either way, he went up to bat again, and again, and with no home run. These almost-wins were wearing on him. He was tiring of the typecasting, of always playing the darker side of humanity, of feeling as if he were phoning in his portrayals... one after another after another. He no longer felt challenged.

Yes, he was picking up a paycheck each time, and the pay was getting better with each new role. Yet Steve Ihnat wasn't in the business just for the money. He had never been in the business just for the money. There was something inside him that required him to be on a stage, and which forced him to reach for an even higher goal with each and every part he played.

He was torn. He had to be an actor but he wasn't finding parts of the caliber he knew he was capable of playing. So he kept on keeping on until he could figure out how to make a change for the better. Steve Ihnat was nothing if not determined to become a bona fide star.

In October he was again on the big screen. He played a hired shooter for the Clanton gang in *Hour of the Gun* (1967), a variation on the story of the fight at the OK Corral, based on the non-fiction book, *Tombstone's*

Steve in *Hour of the Gun*; photo compliments Ihnat Family collection

Epitaph by Douglas D. Martin. In fact, the movie's original title was *The Law in Tombstone*. This telling was intended to be more historically accurate than most of the films done about the same topic. It was filmed in Mexico—the state of Durango, at Estudios Churubusco Azteca Studio, Mexico City; Guanajuato; and Coahuíla.

Steve was signed to the cast by producer-director John Sturges to, as a newspaper clipping wrote, "co-star… for the Mirisch Corp." As Andy Warshaw, a member of Clanton's gang, Steve got a good deal of screen time though, despite the "co-star" newspaper billing, he was most often seen in the background. His biggest claim to fame in this film turned out to be in one of the later scenes when he was, of course, dramatically shot to death by James Garner, a sinister, not-to-be-messed-with Wyatt Earp. They were both part of an all-star cast, some of those at-the-time young actors who would become well-known in later years.

Besides Garner, the cast included seasoned actors Jason Robards and Robert Ryan. Frank Converse would have a successful TV and theater career, and there was also a young newbie by the name of Jon Voight. According to Frank, the experience forced him to be "away from home for a long time sitting on my hands. Or I should say drinking a lot of beer in Mexico."

Years later, Steve spoke highly of Voight in an interview. He called him "an organic actor." He said "the seams that stitch his craft together never show. Now, you might have thought... he really was a kid from Texas. He actually comes from New York State, went to good schools and played Shakespeare." This was the sort of actor Steve truly appreciated, quality acting he felt warranted attention.

Steve and Frank Converse got to know each other even though, in his own words, Frank was, "a snob about the theater because I thought Hollywood actors were nothing to compare." Stage-trained, Frank's heart wasn't with the movies but a job was a job. He was already a veteran of sorts, with his own television show to his name.

Coronet Blue began airing in May of the same year as *Hour of the Gun*, and ended only a few months before the movie hit the theaters. The show would eventually become something of a cult hit among television aficionados, decades into the future, but right then it was not fully appreciated.

Frank wasn't sold on television but he was sold on working, so he took jobs when they came his way. He found himself impressed with some of the actors on this film set and it wasn't long before he changed his tune about those who worked in movies. Steve was one of those actors, and the two started seeing each other whenever their schedules would permit. Frank lived on the east coast, Steve in Los Angeles. When Frank came to California for work, they would get together for coffee or lunch.

Days after *Hour of the Gun* hit the theaters, Steve could also be seen in the comfort of viewer's living rooms on the small screen, yet again. He was once more on the TV show, *Iron Horse*, this episode titled, "The Silver Bullet." Back in the saddle, back in the Old West, and back in the guise of a not-so-nice bounty hunter, this one named Ray McCoy, Steve and three others battled the locals with arson and a terror campaign to force them to give up the man they were chasing.

During that period, Steve went out with a beautiful young lady also regularly seen on television. Bonnie Scott played Judy Bessemer on *That Girl*, the show which propelled Danny Thomas' daughter, Marlo, to notoriety. Bonnie, in 1961, had been the female lead in the original Broadway production of *How To Succeed In Business Without Really Trying* after which she snagged the part of Anne Marie's neighbor. For one season she was a regular. Bonnie was a single mother, fairly recently divorced, and felt she needed to devote all of her time to her children. She worked infrequently in front of the camera from then on.

Bonnie and Steve went on only one date. She recalled they were "fixed up" by a mutual friend, BarBara Luna, then Mrs. Bert Convy. They went to the Bruin Theatre in Westwood. They were actors going to see actors for the sake of entertainment.

Only in Hollywood could two actors go out casually to see a movie at one theater, when down the road or around the corner or on the other side of town, there was another theater showing another full-length movie with one of those same actors in a supporting role.

This was the case here. Sitting in a darkened movie theater next to Bonnie, possibly with popcorn and soda in hand as so many other moviegoers nearby did the same thing, and staring at the big screen in front of him, the celluloid image of Steve Ihnat was at that moment seen on other big screens in and around Los Angeles. Those other filmgoers, with popcorn and sodas in hand, watched a larger-than-life version of him as General Carter in *In Like Flint*.

"Steve's blue eyes were beautiful, like Paul Newman's," Bonnie remembered, "and his voice was mellifluous. His car wasn't memorable—probably one step up from a clunker. I'm pretty sure he opened and closed the car door for me. There was nothing about him I didn't like." Yet for whatever reason, they didn't, as she indicated, have much to say to each other. She didn't even think there was a goodnight kiss.

Bonnie Scott had a lot going on in her life, as did Steve. His career was going full blast, and work took up most of his time. When he wasn't working, and even though he apparently did step out with other lovely ladies now and then, he was becoming more and more enamored of Sally Carter. He just couldn't keep his mind off of her.

The end of the year brought Steve to the small screen again, this time in *Cimarron Strip*, a Western which starred Stuart Whitman. Steve played one of two gun-slinging brothers, with his friend David Carradine as the other. He and Carradine as characters integral to the episode, "The Hunted," (1967) would again cross paths a number of years later. The female guest lead was Jill Townsend who said about Steve, "He was the most intense actor that I had ever met. I had never seen an actor who was more serious and so into the portrayal of his character than Steve Ihnat."

* * *

There was something on television virtually every month, often in multiple shows, with Steve Ihnat's name in the credits. It got to the point where viewers could hardly turn on their set without seeing him on some evening episodic show. He was arguably the busiest actor in Hollywood without his own television show, with no end in sight for him… if that was what he wanted. His phone rang all the time.

Sally said he would sometimes be laughing and shaking his head when he'd pick her up for a date. When she'd ask what was so funny, he'd tell her he was stopped by the police. Again. Why did the cops stop him? Well, he didn't do anything wrong. They saw him at a light, or taking a turn at a corner, or pulling out of a parking space, or something or another. Yet again. It happened so often.

But why?

The police were sure he was a wanted felon. Once they pulled over to the side of the road, checked his insurance and driver's license and really, *really* looked him in the face, they sheepishly realized he was not a fugitive from justice, and they were forced to apologize. Turning all hues of red from embarrassment, they realized he was *that* actor, *that* guy who played the evil, scary fellow they'd seen on TV the night before, terrorizing some unsuspecting community of innocent people.

The officer would invariably laugh nervously and rather than slap him with a ticket and a fine, they asked him for an autograph. Used to all this by now, Steve always took it good-naturedly. As long as he was sure he wasn't signing a summons for court, he gave the cop the autograph.

This became a regular occurrence in Steve Ihnat's life.

His offering for November was another Western, this one with a twist. Set in modern day, "Huntdown" was the first of three *Mannix* episodes he would do. In this one, he was the sheriff of a small town with a big ugly secret, a secret the sheriff and citizens were determined to keep from the outsider, Mannix himself. This wasn't the best show to represent Steve's screen abilities. He was practically able to call in his performance. One write-up stated, "There are several guests but no real guest stars…." This episode focused mostly on Mannix, the man, and the predicament in which he found himself.

As 1967 neared its close, he was on television in a *Mission Impossible* episode titled, "The Astrologer." He traded in his chaps and dusty hat from the Western trail for that other predictable outfit, a military suit, playing as a man from another country. He was again in the skin of another dark personality. As Colonel Stahl, he was the head of the secret police for the Baltic State of Veyska and kidnapped the leader-in-exile. The IMF's mission, which they chose to accept, was to rescue the leader-in-danger from

Steve in "The Astrologer" from *Mission Impossible*

the dangerous colonel. One *TV Guide* notation said Steve played one of the "villains of the week." Nothing new there.

There was also nothing new in how the Cold War continued to be handled in shows such as *Mission Impossible*. These were programs whose storylines became popular as a result of the issues arising post-World War II. On the stage of real world politics, and closer to home, in the United States, national security was a big concern. International politics now more than ever colored not only what everyone read in the newspapers but also what they saw as a part of their daily entertainment. Television producers wanted to reflect reality, but they wanted to do so carefully.

They walked a fine line, most often refusing to name actual countries in their plots. They dreamed up logical but fanciful new bases for their seemingly outlandish storylines of intrigue, espionage, and international backstabbing. Most of those countries at this time, though not all, were in Eastern Europe.

Often the methods employed to do their dastardly deeds seemed futuristic and unbelievable—small knives inside the handles of umbrellas, or snippets of conversation heard and recorded from across a street when there was busy and boisterous activity going on all around, or even the likes of a nearly invisible blow dart tipped with poison to kill the enemy. Yet the truth was that all these things, and so many more, were already in use, and thoroughly plausible. The seemingly unbelievable "movie" world of James Bond wasn't completely imaginary, or completely just in the movies.

All of this explained why an actor like Steve Ihnat, a man with not only the right physical look, but the literal logistical European background, was perfect to be selected time after time to play a general from an Eastern European country at war with the United States; or a double agent attempting to flee a communist government; or a man of dubious history and unclear intentions from a country with a murky relationship with the United States. Steve was a homegrown, playacting spy, and he was so good in the part.

* * *

A week or so after he was seen on TV as a current-day Cold War participant, Steve was thrown back into the Old West, in *Dundee and the Culhane*, a show which didn't last long on the air. The episode was "The Catch a Thief Brief." The show's costumer was Steve Lodge, whom Steve met a few years before on *The Fugitive*, and Steve Lodge dressed him. This time around, they became more familiar with each other while working but they didn't pal around off the set.

Steve's character was a relatively neutral bounty hunter. The episode Steve was in filmed in July 1967 in Tucson. Set in Sabino Canyon, there were ten production men standing nearby as Steve, shirtless in one scene, tugged on a pair of long underwear over his briefs. This was probably the closest he ever came to a beefcake shot in his entire television career, his entire career if not counting *Passion Street USA* from his earliest days.

Steve gingerly sat on a hot rock and waited for his cue. The thermometer the crew kept with them read one hundred degrees. Bounty Hunter Steve prepared to shave. Before the cameras rolled, an assistant director

Steve preparing for a scene in *Dundee and the Culhane*

gave him instructions on how to strop a razor, while at the same time a makeup man lathered his face with shaving cream from an aerosol can, all while he sat on that rock wearing nothing but a pair of long underwear. The glamorous life of an actor.

The scene was run, and Steve was then cut loose for a while. He scraped the lather off his face, put on his shirt, and went off in search of the catered chow line. Along the way, someone asked him to explain the meaning of the show's title. He seemed at a bit of a loss. "John Miles plays the culhane in this... what's a culhane?... well... uh... a culhane is... uh like.... Hey, Mike!" He called to a guy nearby. "What's a culhane?"

Unidentified Mike explained that in Ireland, a culhane was the head man of a family, the chief. This satisfied Steve, and he finished up his chat by saying he was just the guest star in this episode, and the culhane and his sidekick, the Dundee, work to keep his character honest.

The same evening this episode featuring Steve aired five months later, in just a coincidence, all across the country a newspaper column listed numerous viewer raves for the show, asking the network not to cancel *Dundee and the Culhane*. Seemed the viewing public was more intrigued with the show than the bean counters behind the scenes, and the show was taken off the air.

* * *

Steve was found on the tube in no less than seven different appearances in December. He wrapped up 1967 with a substantial role on *Ironside*, playing Peter Zarkov in "The Fourteenth Runner," as a KGB agent who tried to get his hands on a hero of the Soviet Union track and field team who wanted to defect to the United States.

As he was called upon to do again and again, Steve put on an accent as if he was dressing in a comfortable shirt, this time that of a haughty Russian. He was known to be able to mimic virtually any accent and, coupled with his appearance which mirrored the look of many nationalities, allowed him to easily step into the part of "Any Man" from any country. As his visibility ramped up on American television, he found himself specifically playing a good many international spies, particularly from places which didn't necessarily see eye-to-eye with the United States.

In his part as Agent Zarkov, Steve's work was noticed by reviewers. One read the part was "well-played." Another indicated the dialogue between him and Raymond Burr proved to be "biting, jabbing... excellent." It had been nine years since his first bit part on American television. Steve Ihnat had become a household name as an actor who turned in a solid performance no matter who he portrayed, a different role at every turn, and he made his mark on those who made their livings commenting on public entertainment.

His mother worried a lot over the "bad guy roles" her son played so often. She was concerned about how he was portrayed, or how he was portraying himself within these characters. She knew those parts didn't show the world the real person behind the actor. "Why, always, the villain?" she once asked a reporter, as if he could give her a logical answer. "He's a good boy, you know. What I hope is that soon Steve gets to be the one who is kissing the girls."

Of course that reporter couldn't give her an answer. No one really could. One thing was for sure, though. Bad guy or leading lover boy, Steve Ihnat had gained a foothold in Hollywood.

Chapter Five

THE NEW YEAR, 1968, opened with some great press. An article about Steve as a solid actor in his own right, not simply a mention of him as a guest star supporting others in this or that show, was a hefty feather in his cap. The piece called him a "very busy and capable actor" and indicated there were "six unreleased films and one currently in release…" to his credit.

There were unquestionably many working actors in Hollywood, all trying to make their mark and attempting to get their name recognized above all the others, but arguably few could be proven to be as industrious and determined as Steve Ihnat. He was publicly known as one of the most active non-starring guest stars on television.

He started the first month of the year with the title role in "Jed," an episode of *The Virginian*, in a part taped late the year before. Steve was "a young rebel," a gun-slinging cowboy working both sides against each other in a range war between homesteaders and cattle ranchers. One reviewer said of the performance, "Acting honors and the major portion of the story… go to guest star Steve Ihnat…. Ihnat will win your sympathy in his role." Steve had, as usual, proven himself to be a standout.

A regular member of *The Virginian*'s cast was Clu Gulager. These two men would work together in other shows, and would become close friends. Clu had only praise for Steve and his abilities in front of a camera.

"He was what we call a shit-kicker," Clu said of Steve, "instead of just barreling straight through a scene with the lines your roll has, he would kind of hem haw around, kind of look down, like he was sort of kicking some shit on the ground, that's what we call a shit-kicker when you act.

"…the camera likes that a lot. When you work in front of a lens… generally the camera gets upset when you work directly. When you work indirectly, you're an indirect actor, the camera just goes whole hog, the

Steve with Brenda Scott in "Jed" from *The Virginian*

camera just dies with happiness. The camera really likes to see an actor who gives a little space in his acting, a little time. That's what Steve was a master at doing."

Clu had much to say about Steve's ability to get the heart and soul out of the character he portrayed. "Ihnat could take a scene where a guy says, 'Hey Jim, here come here, Y'know...' He wouldn't say it like that. He'd say, 'Jim. C'mere. Yeah. Over here. Uh... Yeah, I wanna talk with you. Uh... yeah.....' All those holes in between the lines, what we call the silence, that's golden when looking at an actor in front of a camera. Steve Ihnat was a master at that kind of acting, what I call do-nothing kind of communication, because that gives the audience, the viewer, a time to interpret what the actor's saying. Ihnat could do that in spades.

"He was also a thinking actor. You got the impression when he was acting that he was extremely with it... intelligent. His intelligence showed when he was acting. Viewers, unconsciously maybe, like to see an actor who had some kind of brain. We're not too sure that actors really have much sense. And basically, they don't. But you have to pretend and give the impression that you do. And you could give Einstein a run for his money in the conversation about relativity. Well, Ihnat had that in spades. He could say a line and you would say, 'Oh shit, that guy's really good.'

"And what did he do? He did nothing. He let the audience interpret, let the viewer work out and figure out what he'd just said or did. Ihnat did very, very little when he acted. By and large, he was not a shouter, he was not a screamer. He kind of slipped up on the viewer."

When Steve was next seen on the screen, it was the big screen. He seamlessly moved from television to movies, and back again. *Countdown* (1967) was

Clu Gulager

made the year before but came out in the theaters in February. Initially titled *Moonshot* when Steve and the rest of the cast were hired, the plot centered on a flight to the moon in a Gemini spacecraft modified for a lunar landing. In real life, there had already been several proposals in the mid-1960s to use modified Gemini craft for lunar orbital and lunar landings, instead of or as a complement to the Apollo flights but the idea was scrapped.

Steve played NASA Administrator Ross Duellan, a tough-talking, take-no-prisoners sort who was there to get the job done. Period. End of discussion. There was no room in his wheelhouse for anything not done by the book. Steve wore his part well, this time working for the United States government rather than against it.

Behind the cameras, he inadvertently found himself peripherally involved in an issue in the making of the film that literally got the director, Robert Altman, fired. From an interview, it was learned Jack Warner didn't like Altman; he thought the other man was a "smart ass," but he gave him a shot at directing the film as a favor to the producer, William Conrad. Warner told Altman he would remove him at the first little thing he did that he didn't like.

Exactly that happened. Altman intentionally interspersed overlapping dialogue among some of the characters, with a good amount of the chatter going to Steve's character, and to Charles Aidman, who played Gus, a doctor for the mission. Altman felt this type of conversation offered more realism; people talked like that in real life. The dialogue of Steve's charac-

Steve in *Countdown*, with James Caan and Robert Duvall

ter, who was difficult and something of a bully, also overrode his secretary's words in a number of places. Studio heads eventually did some re-editing for the final release. Though he lost the job, Altman gained a trademark when this style of multi-layer dialogue became his signature throughout the rest of his career.

And how it was used in *Countdown* was kept in the scene utilizing Steve's character and his aggressive way of overriding other conversations. The movie had a great deal of background realism, as well as factual points. Portions were filmed at the Space Park campus, which is now part of Northrop Grumman Aerospace Systems in Redondo Beach, California. The moon landing was simulated in the Mojave Desert, and NASA fully cooperated in the making of the movie, offering their facilities, including Cape Canaveral in Florida, for location work.

That month a newspaper tidbit showed up in Earl Wilson's syndicated *Mailbag* column which perfectly illustrated the confusion standing starkly between who Steve Ihnat was to the public, those fans who not only watched him regularly on television but who anticipated his next appearance each week, and the media that still hadn't fully picked up on his now fast-growing popularity.

This eager request was sent in by an avid admirer, "Would you please print some information about the handsomest man in television, Steve Ihnat?" The flippant response came back, "He's so handsome, we fail to have any information about him."

The lack of communication between casting directors, the public, and print publicity didn't get in Steve's way in the least little bit. That there was a lack of formal publicity out there about him may have been something of Steve's fault, if truth be told. He didn't believe much in paying for promotion. He was more of an artist's actor rather than a performer seeking the bright lights of Hollywood. He believed his talent should speak directly and wholly for his ability to portray a character. On the rare occasions there was any sort of advertising in print with his name and/or face, it was there for a specific role, and a specific reason. He almost always designed it himself, and saw that it was circulated.

He was in big demand and rarely took time off. This was a fact. The proof was in his nonstop schedule. Next, there was a meaty guest role in *The F.B.I.* which aired in February. The episode was "Region of Peril" (1968) and he played "thoroughly no-good and dangerous Frank Padgett... wanted for kidnapping and murder." Anne Baxter played his hostage, Katherine Daly, whom he captured during a home robbery, a woman he was intent on killing.

Ms. Baxter was a seasoned actor, having been in the business over twenty-five years. In an interview she said about the work, and about Steve, "It's a good script and a good part [sic] just the kind I like. I also had the opportunity to work with Steve Ihnat who is an accomplished actor rugged in the mold of the new anti-hero."

The use of the term, "anti-hero," to describe Steve was a quirky choice. One definition explained that to mean, "...flawed hero and more interesting.... working on the side of good, but with a tragic flaw, or a horrible past, or... selfish and not entirely 'pure.' They can also be working for... evil, but with hidden noble intentions, or other underlying complexities... can be very, very, sexy...."

Whether set in the Old West of the United States, or the shadowy atmosphere of unknown intentions of current international governments, Steve's characters were never one-sided. He played them as one hundred percent human, flawed, fully fleshed-out and believable. His fan base proved time and time again that no one doubted the story behind the man when Steve Ihnat was on the screen.

This was the quality which made him invaluable to casting directors. It was also likely the quality which made it most difficult for him to move from guest star to become the driver of his own show. He was just too good at seamlessly becoming that "Everyman" needed in any and every show on television, and in films, to be pigeonholed into one character week after episodic week.

* * *

Steve did a few forgettable movie roles earlier in his career, and made a decent splash the year before in *Hour of the Gun*. His plan was to move upward in the movie world. He would keep taking on television roles; he

Steve as the madman in *Madigan*; photo compliments Ihnat Family collection

had no intention of turning his back on the small screen, but feeling more and more stifled by what TV offered him of late, he definitely wanted to do more film work.

He was cast in *Madigan* (1968), starring Richard Widmark, Henry Fonda, and a handful of other bankable actors. As the fugitive, Barney Benesch, being chased by Widmark's and Fonda's police characters, Steve played what was called "a perfect twisted and aggressive villain." A viewer stated he portrayed "one the most maniacal killers ever brought to the silver screen and you won't forget him after seeing *Madigan*." A California movie critic said Steve should've been nominated for an Oscar for his over-the-top work. The role was a minor one insofar as the overall script was concerned, even though it drove the plot, but his take on the character etched Barney Benesch into the annals of movie anti-hero history, remembered decades beyond its debut.

One scene in particular has stood out in filmgoer's memory, with impact on one of the film's stars, as well. Steve's character was in bed with a young woman when the police broke in to their room to take Barney away. He pretended to be pleasantly agreeable, thoroughly willing to go with them, but suddenly, he jumped from the bed and lunged at them.

Sally explained in an interview what Steve told her about this moment in the filming of the movie. "Steve scared the hell out of Widmark when he came out of that bed." Richard Widmark, twenty years older than Steve and already a seasoned actor with a film resume dating back to the 1940s, lost it at the deranged look on Steve's face and his sudden movement. Steve was completely in character, thoroughly over-the-top with his actions as a certifiably crazy man. The taping was halted for a few minutes while everyone, particularly Richard Widmark, collected themselves.

When Steve's Old-World European mother saw *Madigan*, she was horrified, not so much, though, by the same thing that halted Widmark in his tracks. Watching the screen, she said, "Oy yoy..." over and over and over, her broken English interspersed with her visibly embarrassed discomfort. She was traumatized to have to look at her son in a bed with a naked woman, and with Steve sitting next to her.

"Ma," he soothed her, attempting not to laugh, "it's make-believe!"

That scene quite upset the film's director, Don Siegel, when it was cut from the final version. There really was a nude girl in the scene. No clothes. He made the movie that way for realism, to intentionally show the nudity, but that was taken out for the general viewing audiences due to concern for the ratings. Siegel didn't like the flow after the cut so he personally re-cut it, and added a line of dialogue which he felt bridged the disruption in the scene, and rearranged it so it made sense, as he felt it was before it had been cut.

There was another movie role for Steve that spring, this one on location in Hawaii. There were worse places to make a movie, and Steve knew it. No complaints from him. *Kona Coast* (1968) was produced by, and starred, Richard Boone. Boone was considered fairly well washed-up by this point, and *Kona Koast* was originally intended to become the catalyst for a television series, and revive his career. He showed executives the pilot; they

Steve in *Madigan* with Richard Widmark, Harry Guardino, and a naked Toian Matchinga

were mildly impressed but it didn't prove to be enough to green-light any episodes to turn it into a bona fide recurring program.

Instead, they offered Boone the starring role in another TV show already in development but yet without a star, titled, *Hawaii Five-O*. Boone was angry about their rejection of *Kona Coast* and he turned them down flat, pouring all his attention into scraping together extra footage to make his TV pilot into a full-length motion picture.

When *Kona Coast* was finally released with the tagline, "IT'S WHERE IT'S AT… The action, the adventure, the excitement of a turned-on world that can't turn itself off!" it didn't capture moviegoer's attention to any great degree. The work simply didn't have the production values of a flashy, high-dollar feature film. The choppy editing and thin script didn't help. Boone's choice to turn down *Hawaii Five-O* proved to be a bad career decision for him in the long run.

While filming *Kona Coast* in the strong Hawaiian sun, Steve got a really bad burn. Whether he was kidding or serious, it was unknown, but Boone told Steve the burn would have never happened if he would have only eaten raw fish. Steve responded definitively, "I'd rather burn to a crisp."

His character, Kryder, was yet another ugly, ugly man, this one of the worst kind of humanity. He was a scuzzy drug lord accused of carelessly luring a girl to her death from an overdose. Steve played the part

Steve in *Kona Coast* with Richard Boone, proving yet again how well he played crazy

with such delighted evil abandon he proved to be thoroughly believable. One review said, "Ihnat is given little to work with in *Kona Coast*, but he makes the most of it with an edge of demonic insanity that makes the viewer squirm." Another wrote that he played the part with "maximum creepiness...."

Even though *Kona Coast* was for the most part considered a B-rated production, Steve's acting was seen as anything but that. Another reviewer wrote of him, "Nods for the best performance goes to Ihnat, the one veteran who seemingly didn't show up primarily for the check and the sunshine. The Czech emigre's effort was in line with the gallery of flavorfully limned villains [he usually played]...."

The Czech émigré? Steve Ihnat, a man who'd lived most of his life in Canada, and who'd lived longer, already, in the United States than he'd ever lived in Czechoslovakia, was still, and almost always, identified only by the country of his birth? This was a curious point which the press would often include, but never explain, when they had even half a chance to do so.

Kona Coast has for the most part been lost to time. Occasionally it will pop up on an old movie channel, and with commentary such as, "The head thug is underrated Steve Ihnat who always gave memorable villainous portrayals in his movie/television forays in the late sixties/early seventies." Whether it was during real-time or many years later, Steve's acting as a dark force has almost always been recognized and noted.

In April, he was in an episode titled, "Turnabout," from *It Takes A Thief*, with Ida Lupino as the other "star" guest star. Ms. Lupino was another celebrated movie actress, in the business since the early 1930s. By this point, thirty-plus years later, she remained well-known, but at the age of fifty, she no longer carried the stronger roles she had in her heyday. Instead, she embraced television and by doing so, was able to continue working regularly. She played a lady scientist in an unnamed Eastern European country, and Steve was her nemesis, the bad guy, Col. Gilveney.

Yet again his character was from a European country which remained without a name, though clearly modeled after the Soviet Union. One reviewer said of him, "Steve Ihnat is impressive, with his handsome face, so adequate for a villain character, maybe more than for a good guy." Was it only his handsome face which made him "so adequate for a villain character?" His ability was uncanny to project the image of someone who unmistakably considered himself above all others—haughty eyes, a curl of disdain to his lips at just the right moment, a tilt to his head which

Steve in *It Takes a Thief*, "Turnabout,"
with Ida Lupino

seemed to portray a sense of pretentiousness.

Even his walk was evenly measured to give the impression of someone who was clearly in charge and, without question, expected everyone to fall in line behind him. All of this despite the fact that, in real life, Steve Ihnat was forever touted as a genuinely kindhearted, generous man in tune with those around him.

It was a quite a feather in Steve's cap to have many of the synopses indicate "Ida Lupino and Steve Ihnat star." Her name still carried quite a punch, and Steve was regularly named in guest star line-ups by this point in his career.

He was delighted soon thereafter to be a part of another *Bonanza* episode—he'd done his first one in 1965. This one was written by Michael Landon, and Steve had the starring male role, a meaty part that would give him a good chance to show his acting range.

"A Dream to Dream" (1968) took six days to shoot, finished up a few days before Christmas, and was released in April. Josh Carter was a wealthy but unhappy horse rancher, an alcoholic, difficult husband and father selling livestock to the Ponderosa after Hoss met him in a saloon.

Hoss, actor Dan Blocker, accompanied Carter to his home, only to find Carter's wife and children miserable with him as the head of their household. When Hoss was invited to stay, they saw how different life might be with a caring man. The story revolved around how Carter handled this upheaval. The story proved to be a kinder and gentler acting opportunity, and one Steve welcomed.

Steve became good friends with both Michael Landon and Dan Blocker. The two men were impressed with Steve's acting, as well as how nice he was to everyone involved with the production. The three remained friends beyond the show's production, in later years visiting each other's homes with their wives for dinner and drinks, and often socializing together.

When this show was taped, however, Steve was not yet married. He was seeing Sally, and they were getting very close. He occasionally dated a few other women but they didn't spark any intense interest in him. People would look at him and consider him to still be a freewheeling bachelor if they didn't know the truth otherwise but, these days, he was feeling more like a happily-attached man. He was a brawny, masculine figure, and women took second and third glances when he entered a room. His heart, however, was taken by a dark-haired beauty who put a spell on him.

That fall, Steve was interviewed by reporter Nathaniel Freedland for a Canadian newspaper. A few years later, Freedland was writing a lot for the *Los Angeles Times*. There were two questions almost always asked of Steve when he was interviewed, and this reporter kept up the tradition... the origin of his name, and its pronunciation and spelling.

"So you learned how to spell my name watching for it on TV credits?" Steve asked Freedland. He was laughing. He explained it was pronounced "eye-nat," a product of his Czech heritage which he refused to change for Hollywood. Steve was proud of who he was and where he came from. He'd gotten this far in spite of his difficult surname. He wasn't about to do anything different now.

He was then asked to describe his career. "It's really a helluva spot I'm in, a killer type waiting for his shot at top roles. Producers don't really want to take a chance on offbeat casting but James Coburn made the jump after years of great villain performances. It's not really any more money I'm after at this point. I just want to be offered the kind of parts that go to a Rod Steiger or an Anthony Quinn."

Freedland asked what his parents thought of his wanting to be an actor. "This was a real close-knit European family, and when I tried to tell them I wanted to act instead of taking over the farm, Mom and Dad literally thought I was crazy."

The reporter wrote about Steve, "Sitting at the outdoor café table on the Sunset Strip, with all the super-gorgeous young men and women parading by, Steve Ihnat is the least flashy looking individual in the vicinity. But on camera, the bull-necked six-footer comes across looking like a meaner and rougher-hewn Steve McQueen." Continuing, the article read, "The 34-year old actor plays tennis and goes skiing to keep in condition, and it shows as he lounges there in the Old World, wearing suede desert boots, beige chino slacks and an open-collared red shirt with cuffs folded up over the sleeves of his safari jacket."

The reporter's description of Steve was an interesting study in opposites to that of the "close-knit European family" image of what his people hoped for him. If he had stayed in Canada and become a farmer, his manly good looks and air of dangerous edginess would have never been cul-

Casual Steve; photo compliments
Ihnat Family collection

tivated, lost in the daily sameness of physical labor. No one would have likely noticed, and keeping in shape would have become a ritual of his regular farm work. Nothing more.

Yet an interview at The Old World restaurant in the hubbub of the big city was, in name alone, fitting. This was a place to be seen, and to leisurely watch Los Angeles go by. Steve's seat on the outdoor patio area looked out over the Strip, with an awning which hung above the tables. Foot and car traffic was constant. Street parking was take-as-you-can-get-it. Businesses hemmed in the restaurant, as well as crowded along the opposite side of the street. Mountains decorated the nearby landscape, with homes of the wealthy and near-wealthy on the hilltops surrounding the area. Steve enjoyed the atmosphere as he leisurely ate his lunch and fielded the questions coming at him.

In answer to one last curiosity, he responded, "No, I've never been married. And that in itself is a commentary on an actor's chances for success in marriage, if you know what I mean."

Within the same period Steve began writing a script brewing in his head for some time. With the odd, unlikely title, *Do Not Throw Cushions Into The Ring*, this story from his heart ultimately became deeply important to him. He knew he wanted to make this into a movie, and take that movie and introduce it to the world. It would be about a year before he was ready to go that far and, in the meantime, he would continue to obediently work for the Hollywood machine as he had for years, day in and day out. Steve Ihnat knew he had to toil in the system if he wanted to eventually be at the forefront of the system himself. And that continued to be his plan.

There were some quickie roles on television which padded his resume, and his wallet, but took little time or effort on his part. Steve had been at the business of acting professionally for a decade, in the town where creating big and small screen dreams was a monumental effort, and squashing those dreams came far too easily. His mark on the industry was already considerable, and that brass ring was dangled in front of him more than once, but was always hanging just barely out of his reach each time. His frustration was beginning to show.

It was nearing the end of that year when Steve was in a television show then known as something of a groundbreaker though, into the future, its splash on the tapestry of entertainment history faded almost into oblivion. *The Outcasts* starred Don Murray as Earl Corey, a white ex-Confederate officer, and former slave owner, and Otis Young as Jemal David, a black ex-Union officer, and a former slave. The storyline took place during the Reconstruction period in American history, and the unlikely pair were thrown together by circumstance as partners in a desperate game of survival. Nothing less, nothing more. No real love between them. They worked on a stagecoach and did what they had to do.

This aired in the late 1960s. Race relations were becoming more and more of a hot button topic. ABC nervously premiered the show but only after pre-screening an episode to "one hundred West Coast negroes, ranging from church elders to black militants," and ninety-eight of them approved the premise. One young militant had a few complaints but his father hushed him by saying, "Listen, son, stop nitpicking. This is the first time I ever saw a Negro cowboy draw a gun and shoot a white cowboy."

In "The Night Riders," (1968) Steve played Jeb Collins, former overseer of Corey's plantation. As the head of a band of hooded men, the group tried to coerce Corey into spearheading an effort to overtake area carpetbaggers. In the process, Corey discovered his former employee had a callous disregard for human life… proving, once again, Steve Ihnat, good guy in real life, could, on screen, play evil to perfection.

Chapter Six

STEVE CONTINUED TO PAY THE BILLS, and that required he take most, if not all, of the parts that came his way. A stand-out opportunity was filmed in late 1968, a role which ultimately became one of his legacy signature characters, quite possibly the role for which he has forever become best known.

Part One of "Whom Gods Destroy," on the now-iconic *Star Trek*, was first broadcast in January of 1969. Steve Ihnat's portrayal of the powerful Captain Garth of Izar, a crazed shape-shifting starship captain known throughout the entire galaxy, firmly centered him forever after in the world of science fiction TV fandom. The somewhat unusual title was based on one phrase uttered by Prometheus in Henry Wadsworth Longfellow's poem, "The Masque of Pandora" (1875). The phrase was, "Whom the gods would destroy, they first make mad."

Steve played Garth with great manic emotion, as one who was once a well-respected and brilliant starship captain but had since slipped into the depths of dangerous madness, "a very intelligent, mostly very controlled madness," as one reviewer put it. Garth's psychosis forced those who had once revered him to now be in great fear of him, and he became an inmate in the galaxy's asylum for the criminally insane.

Steve enacted the part with such flamboyance and outrageous flair that Captain Garth overwhelmed the screen, taking over and dominating both parts of the two-night episode. Sally said Steve chose to play Garth in an intentionally "fey" manner. He wanted the character to appear exaggerated, even outright pretentious, and unquestionably, irrevocably demented. He humanized him for himself and created a defined, deeply personalized sense of who this character was, and was certain he knew how Garth would react amid the situations the script put him in.

Steve as Garth of Izar in "Whom Gods Destroy" from *Star Trek*

Steve's portrayal of this man has remained well-remembered ever since. Reviews came in immediately, and have continued throughout the years. One read, "Ihnat gives a suitably magnetic, over-the-top performance as the insane leader... he really shows what he was capable of in the moments when Kirk was able to break through Garth's madness very briefly." Another said his was, "an elegant and restrained performance," and another, "a showy, scenery-chewing madman role, yet with an undercurrent of dignity, which more fully reveals itself after the character is 'cured' at the end."

And one review eloquently indicated he "...exemplified a convincing manner of psychosis to make credible the concept of a starship captain driven mad by an insatiable thirst for power/revenge." Continuing, the reviewer wrote that Steve embodied "...a formidable sense of realism due to the nuanced fashion with which..." he portrayed Garth. Another indicated what Garth's persona was really all about, and what Steve brought to the captain's personality. "...this particular episode is a favorite... because of Steve Ihnat's broad and somewhat overacted performance. This is not criticism of Ihnat but his part of former Starship commander Garth is a role that calls for it..."

Steve worked closely with William Shatner while he was on *Star Trek*. In an interview in Hamilton, Ontario's *The Spectator* newspaper, he understated the potential for the series, and said of Shatner, "Bill Shatner is a fine actor, and if *Star Trek* can last for a third season, he could be a millionaire. But I found him terribly unhappy. He was tied to a role that was beneath his potential—he was selling himself to it for the money and it was eating him."

Steve understood, and empathized with, this sort of frustration because he was feeling a similar lack of fulfillment. He felt as if he were cast in the same roles, day after day after day, with little chance to really show his full potential. He was making the money, and there was no concern whether or not he could continue to do so, but these standardized roles didn't begin to touch the actor inside him.

This period cemented the relationship between Steve, and his friend, costumer and writer, Steve Lodge, growing bit-by-bit over the years. They crossed paths from show to show, getting to know each other a little at a time, and by the time Steve was called to play Garth, Steve Lodge was, in his own words, "called over to Desilu to replace *Star Trek*'s Wardrobe Set Man for a few days." This allowed them the opportunity to talk off-set about their shared appreciation for scriptwriting, something which would bring them together even closer quite soon.

* * *

The next few months, well into the spring, were busy for Steve as he taped and was seen in TV episode after TV episode. Right on the heels of his *Star Trek* success came another hit for him. "The Mind of Stefan Miklos" from *Mission Impossible* not only gave Steve the chance to play a character sporting his real first name, it offered him a role that would follow him throughout his career as another of his most memorable. This single episode of *Mission Impossible* has since been widely considered, over the years, "one of the most cerebral and intelligent" of the entire series. It was also called "perhaps the most complex and ingenious episode...."

Steve was the title's Stefan Miklos, a brilliant, wily spy for a foreign government, a man with a photographic memory. This trait was one the character shared with the actor himself, and the storyline played heavily on Miklos' ability to see something once and immediately remember it thereafter. Another guest star was Steve's friend, Ed Asner.

One viewer summed up Steve's performance to perfection. "Steve Ihnat is what makes the episode so effective.... He is playing such a richly written and interesting character that totally depends on his ability to visually indicate patterns of thought. I loved watching him think and put the pieces together, loved watching him walk around with a swagger and his pipe as if he owned the world and nothing could outsmart him. Even down to the final seconds when he's convinced the IM Force's attempt to trick him failed. He was simply brilliant and he could communicate so

Steve with Martin Landau in "The Mind of Stefan Miklos" from *Mission Impossible*

much with just the raise of an eyebrow. The tension was tight, and it's all because of his powerful screen presence.... A flawless piece of work."

The Cold War was a well-known subtext woven throughout the history of *Mission Impossible*. "The Mind of Stefan Miklos" was aired during its third season, at a point when the show's creators were utilizing full-tilt the contentious issues at play between the United States and the Soviet Union, and the scripts played around with the nuances of the countries behind the "Iron Curtain." This episode was called, by one reviewer, "a suspenseful game of Cold War chess."

After the show aired, the press came out with a number of tidbits indicating Steve's performance was considered "such a blockbuster" by network brass they were "talking with him about a series of his own." What came of these conversations is unknown. Such a series never happened.

Only a week later, Steve was again on the small screen in an episode of *The Virginian*. "Last Grave at Socorro Creek" had Steve pulling out his in-real-life nonexistent meanness streak yet again as a sadistic killer who embezzled from fellow ranchers the profits of a commonly owned herd of cattle. Another guest in the cast list was Jocelyn Brando, older sister of Marlon Brando.

Steve had the honor of having been bested by Marlon in an ugly brutal fist fight in the movie, *The Chase*, just a few years earlier. His sister was considered by industry insiders to be as accomplished an actress but alcohol, as the years wore on, got in the way of her career, and she ended up forever in the shadow of her younger brother.

Sally was on the set during the taping of "Last Grave at Socorro Creek." In later years, she remembered well the moustache Steve sported for his role as Four-Eyes. He wore glasses with heavy lenses, as well, which gave his character his name, but it was the moustache which had Sally glued to his every move. She said that "curled my toes.... We had an hour between takes... I was not forward but as I said before, he was magic and knocked me for a loop. Fortunately it was reciprocated!"

It was hardly long enough to blink before the viewing public was again treated to Steve's brand of "wrong-side-of-the-law" characters, this time in present-day. In *The F.B.I.*, he played Frank Welles, a man on the F.B.I.'s *Ten Most Wanted* list for the previous five years. The episode, "The Maze," had main characters Erskine and Colby trying to bring him to justice as he entered California from Mexico. Complicating the plot, Welles shot a U.S. Border Patrol Guard, and was trying to avenge the narcotic overdose death of the sixteen-year-old daughter of a friend. Things

Steve, with irresistible moustache, in "Last Grave at Socorro Creek" from *The Virginian*

weren't necessarily as they seemed in this intricate plot, which proved to be the third of seven appearances Steve would make on *The F.B.I.* during his career.

* * *

Canada was paying more and more attention to their "hometown boy," even though his success was coming to him south of their border. Steve was interviewed for the *Toronto Daily Star*'s "Getting Around" column. He was said to be "… the Canadian actor doing the most work on American TV nowadays, and getting the least attention in the national press…." It was as if the Canadian press couldn't resist a slight jab, though. "Ihnat is one Canadian who bypassed the CBC for work. He went directly to Los Angeles…."

When asked about a segment of *Mannix* titled, "End Game," which aired that February, in which he was the lead guest star, Steve explained to another reporter he played a "wiggy professional killer who has Mike Connors locked in a room and is toying with him before knocking him off." His review of the storyline was somewhat humorous even though the episode was called "a chilling suspense yarn." Steve found an offbeat sort of humor in the fact that these were the type of parts he was invariably offered. He was receiving mounting attention for playing characters fighting personal demons, yet this personality type didn't mirror his own. It wasn't his preference, either. This was his second *Mannix* go-round.

There were a few smaller roles here and there before he hit another big guest spot, a repeat on *Gunsmoke*. This was Steve's fifth of six appearances as various characters who floated through Dodge City at one time or another. Here he played a somewhat sympathetic widower who couldn't get over the tragic and violent death of his pregnant wife. Frank Reardon was determined to do the only thing he could think of to rid himself of the pain of his loss. He would track down the last three men remaining of the gang that murdered her. Just so happened they roamed into Dodge. As an old friend of Matt Dillon, Reardon came up against the sheriff in his effort to implement his plan.

The episode's title, "Exodus 21:22," reads from the Bible as, "If men who are fighting hit a pregnant woman and she gives birth prematurely but there is no serious injury, the offender must be fined whatever the woman's husband demands and the court allows." Yet Frank Reardon's wife was mortally wounded, and he felt the offense required her killers to suffer as she had. Steve played the role with a heavy sadness, an aching humanity coupled with a fierce determination that he was justified in killing the men responsible for taking his family from him.

* * *

For the next five months, Steve lightened his work load in front of the camera to focus more of his attention behind the camera. He was ready to take *Do Not Throw Cushions Into The Ring* from concept and on-paper-storyline to that of a completed movie script. There would be a myriad of details required to make this into a bona fide movie.

This didn't mean he would be completely missing from public view. His existing body of work already amassed and in circulation was so large that he was seen just about every week on the tube, often multiple times in any one evening. His ever-growing fan base could easily pick up their television guide and find his name pegged in their favorite TV show as that evening's special guest star. More and more were circling his name in those guides to ensure they didn't miss a single one of his appearances.

Steve Ihnat was nothing if not bold in going forth into new areas of the entertainment world. He was not shy in trying fresh avenues, or in expecting great things for his future. He followed a well-organized plan he set out for himself some time ago, knowing he would want to not only act, but also write, direct and produce. He intended to make movies from inception to completion, and he already had experience in the overall moviemaking process. He'd carefully watched others successful in the field, taking notes of what was required to bring such a complicated effort to fruition. His photographic mind came in handy here and served him well.

Now he was ready to move forward. Still, he wasn't yet able to drop all his acting work and go for broke behind the camera. He put a good chunk of his own money into the effort and amidst all this, he was becoming truly serious about Sally, leaning toward marriage. A union with her would give him a ready-made family, and that would mean he'd have a wife and a child to feed. He needed continuing work to give him income he could always count on. It was important to have many appearances already in the queue before he began to put his movie plan in gear.

Sally was in his movie, as was her daughter, Gaby, who was becoming profoundly significant to him as the days went on. These two people became special parts of his life before he started writing the script. Sally agreed he should take off the needed time and focus on putting together the different pieces of *Do Not Throw Cushions Into The Ring*. The movie was meant to be something of an introspective look into a life similar to his own, although he was quick to tell reporters the story was not autobiographical.

The lead character, Christopher Belton, did his best to maneuver through the maze of being a popular actor in Hollywood, without losing himself or his desire to let creativity flourish in the face of financial independence. Belton's career got to where he could pick and choose his roles, where his wallet was always full, but he rarely woke feeling personally fulfilled by his life's work. Something was missing and he didn't know how to fix the problem.

The title was an obscure reference to the actions in an arena as viewers watched a fight and threw their rented seat cushions into the ring. This did occur during fights—when viewers protested actions in the ring, and when the fight was over, so the cushions could be collected by employees to be re-used in the future.

How's That Again

Actor Steve Ihnat has formed a production company, Tanhi Productions, a nd has set his original, "Do Not Throw Cushions Into the Ring," as his first project. About the name of the company: it's Ihnat spelled backwards. (Or is Ihnat Tanhi spelled backwards?)

Steve forms his own production company

There was a scene in the film where Steve walked through a ring in Mexico but the title held more of a personal meaning to him than it did to that actual scene. His character, and he himself, protested the direction "the suits" from the studios wanted to move his career but he/Chris refused to give in just to make them more money.

One article about him and his new moviemaking venture in the *Los Angeles Times* read, "… he decided a future of two or three decades working as a ruggedly handsome Mike Mazurki (well-known film character actor) wasn't going to be enough." This commentary fit not only Steve Ihnat, but also Christopher Belton, his movie alter-ego.

The United States government required that Steve make a line-up of official arrangements to become the head of his own production company. There were hoops to jump through. He was determined to ensure he and his project were completely legal. He filed papers to create a California Corporation under the name of Tanhi Productions on November 17, 1969, a made-up word which was a playful backwards spelling of his last name. The state number, CO585444, was officially listed as having an office at 11110 Ohio Avenue West, Los Angeles, CA 90025.

Within about a half a dozen years, this very same physical location would become locally famous. The building which housed Steve's business address came down and a baseball field replaced it, covering blocks of land. Bill Lancaster, the author of the script for the movie, *Bad News Bears*, played Little League Baseball on this field and, today, the area is commemorated with a permanent wooden marker to that effect.

When Steve and Sally talked informally of his movie, they would call it *Cushions*. He was the star, and Sally would play his estranged wife, while Gaby was their daughter. He had recently secured his first "outside" actor. In early May, the well-respected Arthur O'Connell was signed to be in the cast. He would portray an altruistic business manager ultimately destroyed by Christopher Belton, his client. O'Connell's name in the cast was a coup for Steve, a solid, public sign of trust in his abilities to make a movie.

By the end of May, gossip reporter Rona Barrett was signed as an "obnoxiously probing lady reporter." This was her film debut. She said Steve treated her "with kid gloves" during filming. Sally remembered Rona seemed to have a crush on him.

Since money was tight, a serious consideration on a budget such as Steve's, each actor agreed to work without pay until the movie came out and proceeds from the sales were accrued. This was an agreement Steve officially worked out with the Screen Actors Guild, just prior to a ruling

Ed Asner

from the Guild which allowed reduced fees for actors balanced by a cut of the film's box office earnings. Steve told one reporter, "This business is up for grabs right now.... Pictures like *Do Not Throw Cushions Into The Ring*—projects that are based more on creativity than on budget—are the coming thing."

Steve was certain this was the only way for him to break out in the industry and prove himself not only capable as an actor but also talented and able to bring quality, original material to life on the screen as a writer and director/producer. He approached his friend, Ed Asner, before he went to anyone else and asked him to take on a plum role as his agent.

He and Ed became closer after working together in past years on a few shows. They liked and appreciated each other, professionally and personally. Ed considered Steve "a jock with a soul." The two discussed Steve's plotline, Steve explaining it with barely concealed excitement. Ed said Steve detailed the plot as a story "about a newly made actor-star [Steve's role], his agent [Ed's role], his separated wife, and a business manager and the business manager's daughter." The action was psychological rather than physical. The conflict came from the character's relationships and needs.

Ed agreed to do it. At the time, he needed the work. "I was doing it to keep busy." The payment arrangement didn't bother him. He said Steve asked him to be a part of his movie because, of course, in his tongue-in-cheek words, "I'm that good!"

In the early stages they would drive around Los Angeles in Steve's Bentley, a beautiful vintage convertible coupe, talking out plot points and using a tape recorder to save their conversations, discussing, changing, adding, and fleshing out the best possibilities for the overall story. Steve would give Ed the gist of a particular scene and explain what he wanted from it, and Ed would let him know how he felt the character should be played.

"He let me improvise," Ed explained. "I gave him the meat of the scene and the meat of his intent, and Steve seemed happy with that." Steve would then go home and play their taped sessions, plugging away on his typewriter to put on paper what he and Ed talked about after each story-line drive-time.

Frank Converse offered thoughtful commentary on Steve's progression from actor to filmmaker. Frank watched Steve's efforts from a distance, marveling at how his friend was able to cohesively put the pieces together. "Steve's view on acting, on work, seemed... just didn't seem all wound up with ambition. He was accomplished. He was in his groove. What fascinated me was that he got this directing, producing thing going on. How the hell did he do that? The mystery was so engrossing. I know a few directors and producers but I don't know anyone who did that from the ground up." Frank mentioned a few actors who moved into directing but who weren't really that similar to Steve in how they made the crossover.

"But their stories were nothing like Steve's. He was younger. Accomplished as a character man. He turned his page. At the time, it just astounded me. My jaw... I was just gaping at him all the time.... He was not... a very singular Hollywood story. I know there are a lot of people then and now who hustle around and get their stuff produced, hook or crook. But he did impress me because he was well into learning the technical side of the business which is so terribly important, especially for a director. So I don't think that for him camera and lighting and cutting were any mystery to him. He was well into the trade."

As *Do Not Throw Cushions Into The Ring* progressed, Sally talked mischievously about the casting process in an interview, and she teasingly discussed her role. "I want to get on a talk show," she said, "and have them ask me: 'How did you get this part?'" She grinned before continuing. "'Well, you'd never believe it,'" she continued her pretend talk show answer, "'I had to sleep with the producer, the director, the writer, the photographer... all of them.'" In other words, her lover, the man of her life.

Frank Converse

Steve put a lot of thought into making this move into filmmaking long before he took the plunge, and he did not go into the venture lightly. He had specific driving factors behind his motivation. So much of him was invested in the project, not only money but, literally, his soul.

"All of a sudden I realized I was putting 100% of my effort into products that were controlled by other people, other factors. No matter how well I acted, there was no guarantee of a successful and satisfying end product. And that's what I needed to put an end to losing choice parts to people who were better known." He started thinking about making a film of his own not long after his arrival in Hollywood. He even wrote two other scripts in addition to *Cushions*.

"Every actor in town is talking about making a film," he added. "The difference with me is that one day I simply told the cameraman what I had in mind and 'let's begin tomorrow.'" And without overthinking it or looking back, he did exactly that. Ultimately, the result became a finished movie. Once Steve made up his mind to do something, he did not waste time and he didn't second-guess himself. From beginning to end, the entire project took him about a year to complete. "I only shot a scene when I was ready to." The entire work was done in sixteen millimeter film, and blown up to thirty-five millimeter film to be shown when it was completed on regular movie theater screens.

Steve was certain he did the right thing for himself. For his career. For the future of what would become his family.

* * *

Life became extremely busy. Except for the few months Steve feverishly focused only on *Cushions*, he still took on role after role, on television as well as on the big screen. His phone never stopped ringing with job offers. Every now and then, a television casting director saw something in Steve beyond the maniacal crazy person, and gave him a role in which he could exhibit other sides of his expansive range.

This was the case in September when he was seen as Bob Stewart on *Marcus Welby, M.D.* in "The Foal."(1969) He and Lynn Carlin played parents of an autistic child who would not communicate with anyone, not even them. Steve always pulled out all the emotional stops when he was involved in a part relating to children, and this time was no different.

Steve and Lynn related well with each other as depressed and troubled parents, at a total loss as to how to handle their son. Doctor Welby

Steve Lodge; photo compliments Steve Lodge

ultimately helped not only the boy but the mother and father, as well. Scenes were full of sensitive moments and character development and, as one storyline overview read, "deserve… attention."

Here Comes The Brides was a family show, with a "lesson-with-a-happy-ending" sort of story in each episode. In his first of two episodic appearances, Steve played "rugged" Sgt. Noah Todd in, "The Soldier," which hit TV screens in October. The youngest of the three Bolt brothers, Jeremy, killed a bear to protect townsfolk who feared for their lives, believing the bear to be aggressive.

Jeremy, and they, didn't know there were two bears in the area. The one they targeted and, sadly, killed, was a trained and gentle mascot, a pet of a nearby Cavalry outfit. This bear had been trained by Steve's character. The one causing all the trouble was wild.

Sgt. Todd started out as angry and embittered, determined to get revenge on Jeremy for killing his bear. Suspense mounted as he tracked Jeremy, intending harm for what the other man did. Yet by the end of the show, all was forgiven and both Jeremy and the sergeant each felt sorry for their respective actions. Goodness prevailed.

Steve Lodge became the costumer for *Here Comes The Brides* in the middle of the first season. When they found they were on the set together, he and Steve greeted each other as old friends which, at this point, they were nearly that. During the time the cameras weren't rolling, they talked about *Do Not Throw Cushions Into The Ring*. Steve discovered Steve Lodge was an excellent sounding board and, in turn, Lodge told Steve about the script he'd written with Dave Cass Sr., a stuntman. Steve was very interested and eager to read it. Lodge agreed, handed the script to him, and Steve read it from beginning to end overnight.

There were few people who didn't fall under Steve Ihnat's spell as an actor. *Here Comes The Brides* story editor, William Blinn, said he was "… a fabulous actor…. One of the things that I observed in Westerns is that a lot of young actors tend to over-analyze this kind of thing. You have to buy the fable, and you have to know what the legend is, and you just have to play the legend. Steve did that…."

Years later, Bridget Hanley, who played Candy Pruitt on the show, was effusive in her commentary on Steve. "I loved Steve Ihnat… I just loved him. He was so talented and sexy, such a wonderful male presence."

Clu Gulager spoke about how women were so often attracted to Steve. His assessment applied Steve's positive physical qualities to how he was able to incorporate sensuality with the best of his considerable acting talent. "He had a certain sexual flow to his talk, to his actions, to his visual image that appealed to women. Did he use it? Yeah, he understood who he was. You can't act if you don't understand who you are. You have to go to your strengths. In his acting, one of his strengths was that magnetic appeal he had to the opposite sex. Because of that, the casting people soon became aware that Ihnat was a valuable property so they used him as much as they could."

Steve was part of a strong supporting cast in yet another episode of *The Name of the Game* which aired just a week later. "Chains of Command" was the story of a small rural prison whose inmates were used as slave labor. Steve played Captain Oliver, involved in an undercover operation to unmask those behind the use of inmates for illegal purposes. Another supporting actor was Dorothy Lamour, a glamorous movie star from a previous generation. Once again, Steve had the opportunity to be a part of a production which included a star of yesteryear. The acting was considered "superb" by many reviewers.

* * *

Steve earned about $70,000 in 1969 as a guest actor, acting on just about every American TV show on the air, a sizeable sum by most any Hollywood standards for an actor without his own starring vehicle. He was seen almost every evening on one show or another. He was repeatedly called back to guest on the same shows, as well as cast in new ones, and he was never out of work.

Yet he was tired of so often being seen as the bad guy, the heavy, rarely given a chance to expand his range out of that identity. "My career is at the phase where everybody sees me in a part and says, 'Oh yeah, there's whats-isface playing another whacked-out killer.'" This was wearing on him.

It was that intensity Steve employed in his acting, his determination to fully engage himself and climb right inside the fictional head of his character, and live there, intrinsically knowing how to be that individual in every facet, which made him unforgettable and got him so much work. It was also, unfortunately, probably that intensity and passion which lent his brand of acting so well to the seedier side of humanity. This was both his blessing and his curse. He continued on with television, rarely turning down an offer, as well as taking on more movie roles as they came his way.

Steve and Sally were falling comfortably into step as a couple. Things felt right when they were together. She remembered many good, and funny, times. One particular evening, they were at the house off of Laurel Canyon, an old hunting lodge which Steve shared with his friend, Brad.

Sally said Steve was "just furious about something. He kicked a speaker or... it seemed to me it was a speaker, showing his anger. He was furious and his legs went out from under him and he went down, fell flat on his ass. Well, I'll tell you, that's all I needed! I dissolved into laughter. I was bent over, weeping from laughter. He kind of got up, didn't look at me but started to smile, then giggle. I asked him if he felt better after that. He said, 'Other than my ego, I feel better.'"

Just before Christmas, Steve had a solid lead guest star role on *Then Came Bronson*, in "Two Percent of Nothing." As Royce MacLeod, he was a near-destitute, and desperate, oil wildcatter trying to get the well to produce before his bills, piling up fast, overwhelmed him completely. The show was filmed in the hot desert sun outside of Phoenix, and Patricia Quinn played his wife, one lonely woman amongst a group of unhappy and lonely men.

In his second-to-last television appearance for 1969, he was seen in "The Prey," a segment of *The F.B.I.*, playing Carl Beaumont, a conman of the most despicable sort who, along with his partner, a pretty nurse, made a living robbing elderly invalids. She made friends with the unsuspecting victims,

Steve in *Then Came Bronson*

luring them into her confidence, and Beaumont, acting on her insider information, stole the valuables, knowing exactly what to take and where to find each item. This proved to be just another example of Steve playing the dark side of a man, and doing it so believably.

He ended that year, predictably, in the skin of yet another foreign military-type killer trying to sell top secret materials to an enemy nation. As Major Paul Johan in "The Amnesiac," from his last of three appearances on *Mission: Impossible*, he was a malevolent man playing around with materials used for nuclear development. Steve once again put in a fine performance similar to any which he had played many times before. This was but another paycheck for him.

He and Sally went to his hometown in Canada for Christmas. His parent's home was always completely decked out for the holidays and his fast-growing fan club excitedly awaited his visit. The club's president, Joan French, and vice president, Irene Chapman, and some of the loyal members, would attend his family Christmas party, and Steve always enjoyed their company. This year, a young lady of about eighteen was part of the invited group. She was going to play her guitar and sing for the assemblage. She wasn't thought to be shy, and she was ready to have her moment in front of everyone, including the guest of honor, Steve Ihnat. She didn't yet know him personally but looked forward to meeting him.

Along with the rest of her audience, Steve sat politely, quiet and attentive, watching and waiting for her to begin her concert. She looked him in the eyes, fumbled with her guitar, and cleared her throat a few times. Looking away suddenly, and then glancing down, she finally shook her head and said quietly to the person beside her, "He's so sexy! I can't play when he looks at me so handsomely!" She put down her guitar and walked away from her makeshift stage without a single note of music played or a word sung.

Steve managed to stop her in her tracks before she even started, and he had no clue he'd been the cause of this aborted recital.

Chapter Seven

IT WAS NOT ONLY ON THE VERGE of a new year, but also a new decade. It also seemed as if Steve's career was moving into an expanding space. He wasn't only a guest star these days, he was most often *the* guest star, the lead actor driving the action in many featured episodes. He would get fan mail, lots of fan mail, addressed to any of the studios which put out the different shows in which he appeared. Fans who enjoyed his acting simply didn't know how to get hold of him otherwise.

He was always happy to read those letters. Some were touching. Others were outrageous. Almost all of them really tickled him. One letter, in particular, stuck out in his mind, and while laughing, he told his fan club friends about it, reading it to them verbatim. *"Dear Steve. I am writing this to you in bed. Wish you were here...."*

When he was seen these days in a television series, it was watched each week by dedicated viewers who had already scoured their television guides looking for Steve's name in each show credit, and who knew he'd be on that show, on that night. There was now a happy suspense amongst them, an eager anticipation to see Steve Ihnat on TV. Viewers expected to see him on their favorite shows. On any TV show, for that matter.

This gave him the opportunity to be seen in American living rooms almost any night of the week, and his face was familiar to the television viewing audience. His face was familiar, his acting was appreciated and anticipated, and the public wanted more of him. This fact didn't escape the awareness of television executives and they took dedicated notes.

Yet somehow, this wasn't exactly what Steve Ihnat wanted. He wasn't ungrateful but his dissatisfaction with the fabric of the industry and what studio heads seemed intent on molding him into was becoming more pronounced. What they wanted to see him become within the industry wasn't what he wanted for himself.

At the risk of alienating some of those executives who gave him the parts he received so regularly these days, he told a reporter that though he found some of his TV work satisfying, for the most part "it's the patronizing medium, providing the pap that it thinks the public wants." The reporter wryly observed Steve didn't hesitate to bite the hand that fed him.

Steve believed Hollywood made its product for one reason, and one reason only. Money. The final result had little if anything to do with art, or talent, or the best of the best. It was all a financial proposition in the final count.

"If you're in a film that makes a lot of money, you have the world in your hand," he told the reporter. He often used the word "cosmetic" to describe the glamour Hollywood once held as its ultimate doctrine but which now was, in his opinion, in a fast decline. The "Beautiful People" of the "Dream Factory" had it made, and if they could pump in more money for the studios, the Tinseltown world was theirs. The publicity mill sealed the deals and convinced the movie-going public that make-believe was real and forever happiness was but a movie ticket, or a television screen, away.

There was no question Steve Ihnat owned the talent to make it in the entertainment industry. There were too many producers and directors ringing his telephone these days to question that as fact. But was he willing to play their game long enough to become one of them? Steve's argument was, "The least prerequisite in Hollywood is talent. Talent has never been important except when it stands out so vividly that it hits you in the face." He went back to his original argument, with more force this time. "Business is really a whore. The whole thing behind Hollywood is money."

Steve was fast becoming a cynic, though in his brighter moments, he tried not to give in to those sentiments. Those moments were, unfortunately, becoming less frequent.

* * *

Work completed late the previous year hit the small screen just after the beginning of February in 1970. In "Fright and Flight" from *Medical Center*, Steve was once again a worried parent, father of a young student who years earlier was in a motorcycle accident, causing her blindness. Doctor Gannon suspected the cause of her ailment to be hysterical blindness, and the story centered on him trying to get the girl into treatment with a psychiatrist. The drama unfolded as her parents created an unexplained resistance.

If Steve were to have categorized the three most called-for characterizations he usually played, undoubtedly the "bad guy" would have been first on the list. The second was at the opposite end of that spectrum; he was often one of the "good guys" who upheld the law. And, as he added a few years to his age, he was called on to portray a father.

Yet he was never any ordinary father. Almost always he played a parent in anguish, finding himself in some sort of torment over his child's condition or situation. This seemed to speak to his ability to internalize his emotions and relate his feelings in a believable fashion. Steve wasn't a surface actor. He went down to the core. Ed Asner said there was "another person inside. He walked through life cryptically." It was that cryptic quality which seemed to give Steve Ihnat the ability to pull from within whatever emotion might be needed at any given moment to realistically portray a wide array of characterizations.

Barely a week later, TVs across America were again tuned into a show featuring Steve. His personal history continued to give him the perfect background for the international characters he was so often called on to portray. The man born in Czechoslovakia, learning English in a rush after emigrating from his homeland to Canada, and then taking on the United States as a surrogate country in order to have the career he wanted since his childhood, this gave him a unique place in the minds of casting directors.

Paris 7000 was a show built out of the ruins of a previous creation called *The Survivors*, originally written for Lana Turner, Kevin McCartney, and George Hamilton. *The Survivors* premiered on ABC in September of 1969 and immediately the reviews came in, blasting the production from every angle. Ratings were bad. Personality conflicts raged behind the scenes. Nothing went right.

The network was, however, committed to a full season so they came up with a solution which allowed them to fulfill their obligation. The format and title was drastically changed. The earlier stars were dropped, except for George Hamilton. He was given the lead for what was now called *Paris 7000*. Ratings for this were better than for the original but still were anemic. The series in its rebirth proved to also be short-lived and aired for only ten episodes, from late January to late March.

In his guest-starring role, Steve found himself playing an East German officer alongside actor, John Van Dreeland, in the fourth episode, "Journey to Nowhere." This was a paycheck job, little more. The role did, however, exhibit his capably long, and ongoing, reach in portraying an individual involved in secret dealings between a foreign government and the United States.

The next month, Steve had another go-round on *Here Comes The Brides*. It had only been five months since he'd last been seen on the show. His work was well-received then, and this time, though his part was once again a character who was emotionally rough around the edges, he was given the opportunity to stretch his range.

In "Absolom," as the uncle of a young boy who was a deaf mute, played by Mitch Vogel, Steve as Oliver Tray came to town to have his nephew put in an asylum. There was no love lost between him and the boy as the story opened. Tray believed the young man couldn't be a part of general society due to his violent behavior. The Bolt brothers believed otherwise, and wanted a chance to prove their case before a court was convened to give his uncle full custody.

Steve was again playing against a young actor. Though not a father in this part, he portrayed a father figure, allowing him to utilize a range of emotional skill never evident in his darker, more menacing characters. By the end of "Absalom," Steve gave the audience a heavy dose of paternal sentimentality, and viewers could believe he was father material, which was exactly what the script called for him to be.

Steve worked on the movie, *Zig Zag* (1970), the year before. With shooting which started in August of 1969 and finished by December, the production was originally titled *False Witness*. When it debuted in international theaters, specifically in Australia, it retained the original title.

In the United States it came out as *Zig Zag* in late April, starring George Kennedy as a dying man, Paul Cameron, who framed himself for kidnapping and murder so his wife and daughter could get reward money for his capture. His plan backfired and he was prosecuted, finding himself up against Assistant District Attorney Herb Gates, aka Steve Ihnat. Also in starring roles were real-life husband and wife team Eli Wallach and Anne Jackson. Even though this movie would seem dated years later, the storyline was lauded in its time as "edge of the seat" material, with many viewers "dumbstruck at the ending." Others called it "an absorbing thriller."

Filming took place at locations all around Los Angeles—the Lincoln Heights City Jail, which was soon to be demolished; the ruins of Santa Anita racetrack; the Venice canals; and the Los Angeles Civic Center. This was one of the first "big-budget" films in a considerable amount of time filmed entirely on location in the Hollywood area. Local high-dollar moviemaking had been in a slump for some time.

Steve's career took an intentional backseat in importance for him in May, if only for a short time, when he made the plunge and married his sweetheart, Sally Grajeda. Known professionally as Sally Carter, she was unquestionably the most beautiful and stunning woman he'd ever known. He was smitten with her since the moment he laid eyes on her, and they'd been together ever since.

Sally adored the way Steve proposed. Simple but so sweet. They were in her kitchen, and he said, "I wish you would be my wife and marry me. I want to be Gaby's daddy, and your husband." The fatherly type part he had taken on more and more on screen was now a real-life role for him, one he wholeheartedly embraced. He loved Gaby as his own.

Their wedding was held at the Little Brown Church in Studio City. This church, located on Coldwater Canyon Avenue, had a celebrated history, one which seemed to fit in with the fabric of Steve and Sally's relationship. The doors opened in the 1930s, the vision of one minister who wanted to see a refuge in the city open at all hours for people with spiritual needs. It was something of a favorite for the Hollywood community, and one of its most famous weddings was that of Ronald Reagan and Nancy Davis.

Steve and Sally's wedding ceremony; photo compliments Ihnat Family collection

Sally wore a long, flowing white dress with bell sleeves and a peach-colored wide ribbon around her waist. She sported a crown of delicate flowers in her beautifully-coiffed, wavy upswept hair. Steve had on a dark pinstriped suit. His hair was a bit longer than how he usually wore it, curling upward a bit in the back, and he had that mustache which Sally loved. She carried a bouquet of white and peach flowers, and Steve had a boutonniere of one white flower in his suit jacket lapel. Both of them sported wedding bands.

Steve's Best Man was his good friend and roommate at the time, Brad Bradbury. Sally's Maid of Honor was Sheryl Trunzo, her best friend, whom she had known since junior high school. Good friend, Canadian actor Larry Dane was there, as was Sally's brother Wayne Grajeda and his girlfriend, and Steve's parents. There were a handful of other guests.

Accompanying Steve and Sally throughout the ceremony and reception was the adorable little Gaby, Sally's daughter by birth, and Steve's daughter by heart. She was so happy Daddy Steve was marrying her mommy, and she was now his best girl. Gaby and he were nearly inseparable, and he treated her as his own. She wore a knee-length, long-sleeved white dress, with a large ruffle at the neck and another at the hemline. Her legs were covered in white hose, with white socks and shoes.

Steve's adoration of Gaby was clearly evident to anyone who watched them together. In their post-wedding ceremony photos, Steve held the young girl in one arm with his new wife on his other side as he and Sally kissed. Another picture showed Steve standing next to Sally with Gaby in front of him, his hands gently resting on her tiny shoulders. As soon as he and Sally said, "I do," the three of them were a family, a family which Steve Ihnat was completely ready and delighted to take on.

He moved seamlessly into married life and fatherhood. Steve would drive Gaby to school in the mornings before he and Sally went to work. He would make that drive, as Sally said, "a lot. Gaby would always want to go with him." Sally would be right behind him as they both left the house in their respective cars. During this period of time, when she was about four years old, as Sally remembered, Gaby had a habit of acting as if she "was a puppy." Sally would watch through her front car's window and see her daughter with Steve, both of them in the front seat of Steve's car, as their cars drove down the hill.

"In those days," Sally explained, "we didn't have seat belts. I could see her, up in Steve's face, from my back window, and she'd be licking his face and pawing his shoulder."

After the wedding, the Ihnat family; photo compliments Ihnat Family Collection

As Sally explained, this was a stage Gaby went through. In her little-girl mind, Gaby decided, for whatever reason, she was a little dog. She was on her knees next to Steve in the front seat, licking him and gently pawing him as a puppy might.

Sally was forever amazed at his patience. She added, "He'd be very stoic in the car.... His head was going straight forward. He wasn't playing back with her then. . ." as he drove. She could see he wasn't, but he wasn't yelling at her, either. Steve went right on paying attention to the road, never missing a beat, never looking distracted, but not once telling her to stop. He managed to handle the task at hand without being sidetracked by the active child next to him.

How he was able to handle a young child so well always amazed Sally. He never before had children of his own. He saw his nieces and nephews often and always enjoyed playing with them, and was always very present with them. His niece, Brenda Mordue-Humpries, adored him and said he knew what to say and do with her and her siblings and cousins. Sally said when he was with children, Steve gave them his full attention. Not only the kids had fun, but Steve did, as well.

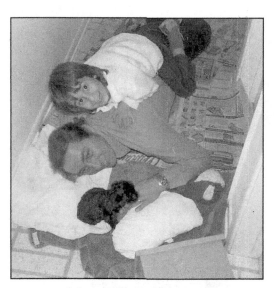

Steve with little Gaby and their dog, Bootsie;
photo compliments Ihnat Family Collection

She remembered one of his regular habits. "When Steve worked, every single day he worked, he would come home to dinner with us, and then go back to the studio to edit. During dinner time, he would get down on the floor and wrestle Gaby, the two of them would wrestle and wrestle. Sometimes he'd win. Sometimes he'd let her win. And of course, Bootsie Ihnat [their dog] would always be in the mix. The three of them would be flying around the floor. Bootsie was a curly black, part poodle, part… he was a mix. He was a puppy, not grown." She laughed. "There were three puppies on the floor, rolling around."

*   *   *

That October, Steve was again called on to put on an accent and a period costume. This time he was an Englishman, in an episode of *The Young Rebels* titled "Suicide Squad." He played Sgt. Nobby Whipple in the period of the American Revolution, disguised as a member of the Continental troops in a stolen uniform. In truth, he was a Brit trying to assassinate General George Washington.

His friend, Steve Lodge, also worked on *The Young Rebels*, and this is where the writing partnership between him and Steve Ihnat really took form. They compared the progress of their respective projects—Steve's film, *Cushions*, and Lodge's script, *Honcho*, which he'd just completed with Dave Cass. The next day, Lodge said, "he asked me if I'd be interested in writing a rodeo script with him."

Do Not Throw Cushions Into the Ring had a special screening at the academy Award Theatre for members of the Academy of Motion Picture Arts and Sciences in early October. Steve arranged everything with little assistance. Members were required to present their membership cards to be admitted and were allowed to bring one guest. Reviews covered the gamut. Most felt the production was a lofty effort, well-done yet possibly a bit too long and artsy for general audiences. Steve was heartily applauded for his first foray into moviemaking, and especially for putting together such a cohesive effort on a minimal budget.

Steve Lodge readily agreed to write with Steve, and the two men immediately began working on opening scenes of what would ultimately become

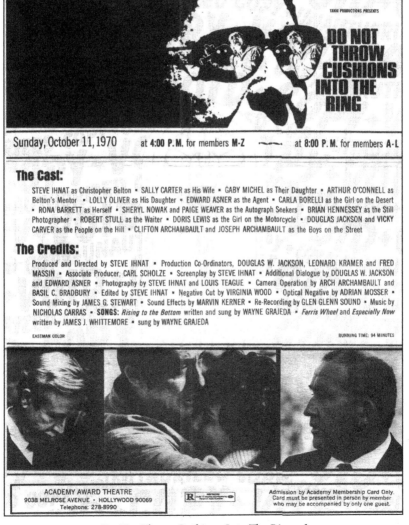

Do Not Throw Cushions Into The Ring ad

known as *The Honkers*. They spent about four weekends formulating the story together, and then they got it on down on paper, in between working their respective jobs as actor and costumer. On the weekends, they would sit together by Steve's pool, hashing out their rough draft. During the week, Lodge would take the draft and type out what they put together.

The Honkers poster

It took them about a full month, and then a bit more. Once that stage of the process was completed, they went looking for a rodeo to attend where they could soak up the color, the atmosphere, actual details of such an event, and the announcer banter heard at all rodeos. Steve wanted to star as well as direct this film, so the lead, Lew Lathrop, was written with him in mind. He and Lodge intended this to be an "inexpensive, personal movie." They originally titled it *Home Town Boy* but Steve decided that didn't have the right ring. They ultimately changed it to *Honker*, which evolved into *The Honkers*. The term, in rodeo jargon, referred to an animal, or in this case, an individual, specifically the character, Lew, who was difficult to keep under control.

Steve had managed to put together *Do Not Throw Cushions Into the Ring* on a shoestring budget which impressed studio bigwigs when it came time for Steve and Lodge to peddle *The Honkers*. Movie industry insiders were shocked to learn a newcomer to filmmaking, Steve Ihnat, did what was considered "the impossible." He made a decent film, from start to finish, for a lot less than one hundred thousand dollars. Even that was considered a lean budget in many circles, and the amount of money Steve managed to work with was unheard-of in those days.

Steve's agent sold the script to United Artists in a month. The Levy-Gardner-Laven production team was attached to the project, giving Steve a serious second look for his attention to detail, believing this upstart, actor-turned-film writer and director, just might have something going for him. *The Honkers* was intended to be a test for the cocky-but-talented industry insider, meant to show whether or not he had what it took, the staying power, to make it behind, as well as in front of, the camera.

The only real downer in the entire deal came when United Artists announced that Steve would not play the lead. They wanted someone else and because they were footing the bill, they got their way. James Coburn was given the part in March of 1971. Steve was disappointed but he got over it. He was a professional and he saw where this overall experience could take him. Focusing all his energies on the sizeable job of director, he poured himself into his work. He and Lodge took Coburn to a real rodeo so he could be up close and personal with a true rodeo experience. Born in Nebraska and raised in relative middle class in California, Coburn wasn't familiar with the lifestyle of a rodeo performer. He played more than his share of Western characters, however, and that part of the role came easily to him.

On the set of *The Honkers* with Slim Pickens giving Steve a neck rub; photo compliments Steve Lodge

Slim Pickens was soon cast and used to the top of his ability in a supporting role, possibly in the best part of his career. He was allowed to play to his dramatic side as a rodeo clown, his actual profession for many years before becoming an actor. Anne Archer and Lois Nettleton were cast as love interests. This was Anne Archer's first film role, and she played a Native American. She and Sally ultimately became good friends. Filming was scheduled to begin in May, and shooting would be entirely on location in Carlsbad, New Mexico, where the rodeo was still a regular way of life.

Slim, according to Sally, "adored Steve." She said they got along famously. She and Steve and Gaby would go to Slim's house and spend the day, riding the horses and, surprisingly, the jackasses, too. Sally told an outrageous story which sounded as if it came straight out of a cowboy film.

She and Gaby rode a donkey during one visit, with Gaby seated on her lap. "This jackass suddenly took off and… as far as he was concerned, [it was like he said] 'I want to get back to the barn and eat!' All of sudden, he was running like the wind. I was terrified. I started screaming and was holding on to Gaby." As she re-told the story, Sally was laughing, though she hadn't been laughing when she was on the back of the donkey.

Continuing, she related, "Steve saw this, and he and Slim took off after us. We must've looked like we were in a movie, and two cowboys were coming to save the damsel in distress with the little girl on her lap. This jackass—and I keep saying that because he would try hard to get me off. I would stuff myself down and hold onto Gaby as hard as I could. He absolutely was going to get me off his back! Finally Steve got hold of the reins. He was doing a movie move! Slim came up the other side and the two of them managed to stop him. It was like the hero, the guy in the white hat, came to save the damsel…. It was certainly an experience. I got off that jackass and never got back on!"

The Honkers took complete advantage of the unencumbered Western landscape of New Mexico in all its glory. A reviewer said it had "an authentic feel with the necessary level of grittiness and good rodeo footage."

To simulate a championship bull ride, the special effects people put Jim Coburn, as his character Lew Lathrop, on a fake bull using a fulcrum with springs, anchoring it to a six-wheeled ATV. That was driven by the stunt coordinator over bumpy ground. Coburn was followed with a long-focal lens showing only a close-up of his face. The background showed the rodeo grounds.

Steve's sister, Emily Mordue, said her daughter, Brenda, started singing when she came out of her womb. As a child, she would sing from morning until night, climbing out of her bed with a song on her lips. One of Brenda's favorites was "Wichita Lineman" by Glen Campbell. She had a habit of roaming the family farm and picking wildflowers, singing as she picked and played amid the fields.

Uncle Steve was well aware of his niece's penchant for making her own music, and she was good at it. During a visit to his parent's home while he worked on *Honkers*, he wanted to get Brenda to sing for him. He took a tape recorder and followed her outside, asking her to sing "Wichita Lineman." He put the microphone in front of her, expecting her to go to town on the song. Nothing. As she explained, "I was a bit shy and un-

On the set of *The Honkers* with Steve riding the simulated bull;
photo compliments Ihnat Family Collection

prepared and nothing came out of my mouth." She said he kept trying and would rewind the tape recorder to capture her sweet voice. Nothing. "I felt really sad that I disappointed him," but she just couldn't sing at that moment. Looking back on the experience, Brenda surmised that "he might have used my voice on the soundtrack from what I believe so I really missed a great opportunity."

What began as a small, personal script written by two men who came to know each other bit-by-bit on television sets, became a Hollywood production costing 1.5 million dollars, a tiny budget by industry standards. The filming included a parade created especially for the movie. Local folks, 17,000 of them, turned out to support the choreographed event—sixty-plus entrants, including bands, floats, and horse groups. To film this, five cameras were used, and the parade ran around the block so it could be shot in a loop to gain the required amount of footage.

One reviewer, Bruce Kogan, said of the finished film, "Steve Ihnat really captures the ambiance and feel of the rodeo as an American institution." *The New Biographical Dictionary of Film* (1975) called it ". . . an engagingly modest rodeo story." *Playboy* magazine wrote Steve and "script collaborator, Steve Lodge, invested their first joint effort with plenty of warmth, behind-the-scenes color, and the do-or-die enthusiasm that is often lacking in old, experienced hands."

Clu Gulager was impressed with how in tune with the overall creation process Steve was behind the cameras. His skills, he felt, went far beyond that of an actor. "Ihnat had a large head," he explained in his humorous, nonchalant fashion. "It looked like his head was full of brains, and brains were just oozing out. I don't know how smart Steve was. He made a movie. He was one of the actors most sought-after in America."

Then Clu's voice became almost wistful. "I had the impression that Steve always wanted to do something better. By that I mean, he was doing a television show, which was very important in Ihnat's day. He wanted to make a movie instead. He always wanted to be on the other side of the camera, telling the actor, let the actor work, let him do his thing. That was my impression with Ihnat. I never thought he was just an actor. I always thought… there was something going on in that big head of his… I couldn't comprehend, that was beyond me, and as it turned out… that was true."

His thoughts on *Honkers* were clear. "It's absolutely, totally impossible, to make a motion picture. It's something that's so complex, so complicated, that you can't do it. Well, Steve made a film. A commercial motion picture. Very good one. About cowboys. Rodeo. Well, I'm a cowboy myself. A rodeo guy. His film was extremely authentic. He captured some things most Westerns about cowboys don't."

* * *

As *The Honkers* was in production, well on its way to public viewing on the big screen, TV viewers turned on their sets to find Steve looking back at them, as usual, from the other side of the small screen. On *Mod Squad*, he played Tom Blake, a "hard-nosed ex-cop" just returned from Vietnam. The episode was, "Search and Destroy." (1970) His character received a phone call from his younger brother, telling him he witnessed a murder. His brother was killed immediately after that call in a suspicious car "accident." The murderer, Blake discovered, was an undercover cop.

Blake was unaware there was an undercover operation behind the scenes and his brother had walked in on a narcotics smuggling operation. He was determined to avenge his brother's death, with or without the law on his side; he had no idea who or what he would battle to get his

Steve with Tige Andrews on *The Mod Squad*

revenge. Pete, Linc, and Peggy had to save him as well as take care of the bad guys. For once, Steve did not play one of those bad guys. Rather, he was one of the characters at their mercy and in need of help, an interesting change of pace for him and his acting talents.

November brought Steve nearly back-to-back television roles. Always notable were those that were different from the norm, not only for Steve as an actor, but unusual for TV, in general. Even somewhat brazen for the time. On *Bracken's World*, Steve took on the role of actor Larry Sims, an occupation with which he was obviously quite experienced. This actor was a very well-known movie star, already in the business long enough to become jaded and bored with his lot in life.

The episode was titled "Nude Scene," and Eva, his co-star, played by Lois Nettleton, was a married woman, a mother and respected actress with a lot of film work to her credit. In this part, she played opposite Larry in a role very much out of the norm for her. She would have to be nude in what she was told was a "relevant" love scene between them. She had agreed to the part, and the rest of the movie was nearly completed, yet when it came time to film the nude scene, she vacillated. Eva wanted to change her mind; she was concerned over what her husband and children would think. This created a problem for the producer. The film was too far in the can to change, and he was forced to rely on her co-star to help her through her concerns. Larry cajoled her into completing her obligation.

This was an emotional and introspective script, requiring internalization rather than physical action on the part of the actors. Steve handled his role as a man who felt he was beyond his prime, not certain if he was in good enough physical shape to bare it all on film. He ran with the gamut of his own feelings. Watching his co-star go through her own emotional agony, he realized he was also unsure if he wanted to get naked on camera any more than she did.

Steve dealt with his character's feelings by masking them with growing frustration as he tried to be patient with Eva. He let his emotions get raw, almost boiling over before he would manage to corral his temper. When he would get to the edge, he'd step back and force himself to find the heart and gentleness necessary to help her through the sensitive nature of their work, ignoring his own uncertainties.

Steve and Lois Nettleton had great natural chemistry. A friendship developed off-camera between him, Lois, and Sally. The "nude scene" was filmed for the show in two versions at the request of the network. One was a view from the back, showing Lois only from the shoulders up, and the second showed her from the waist up, with neither one exhibiting anything that in today's world would be beyond a G-rating. Still, the show aired only the more modest shoulder view.

For the next month, Steve popped up on TV in a number of forgettable shows, the roles nothing more than the rehashed characterizations he usually played, with storylines changed here and there—different time periods, situations altered, locales from east to west. That didn't vary the appeal of his acting. He always put out a good performance, no matter the material in which he performed.

In late December, Steve put a different spin on a stock story. Again this one centered on him as a father figure, with a daughter as the main character. The show was *Gunsmoke* and the episode was titled, "Jenny." This was his last of six appearances and quite possibly his best. Steve played Jenny's father, Lucas Pritchard, a wanted outlaw. Jenny was a ten-year old girl who came to Dodge City alone by stagecoach to find her father.

The story surrounded the relationship between the young girl and her father who agreed to go to trial without causing trouble, but only if he could have two days with her before he turned himself in. The deal was made without the local judge's agreement. Steve played Pritchard as a sorrowful dad, deeply ashamed over the life he led and bothered that his daughter now saw him as he really was, not as she desperately wanted him to be.

His ability to interact with young actors didn't fail to shine through as he played opposite his co-star, Lisa Gerritsen. One review said of him, "As the regretful dad, skillful Steve Ihnat displays quiet strength in a cliché part...."

The following spring, after a few months of television appearances which popped up on shows which either didn't have staying power or which were simply forgettable, Steve was again able to sink his teeth into a role which suited him well. Considered by some to be another of his legacy roles, in the vein of his "psycho" portrayals, the person of Mr. Ganns on *Bonanza*'s "Terror at 2:00" (1971) gave him leeway to explore the tortured soul of a man who hated the Indians, any Indians, a man determined to exterminate them as a race from the face of the earth. The script was written and directed by his friend, Michael Landon, and it's possible Landon considered Steve's acting depth as he created Gann's character.

One reviewer said Steve was a "study in fanaticism," and "really something to watch." A brief scene deep in the middle of the episode allowed Ganns to slip into a moment of sanity as he spoke to a young boy in his hotel room. The gentle play of emotions crossing his face as he considered the fate of this child, a fate he himself was willfully creating, gave insight into Ganns' troubled psyche… as well as this actor's extensive bag of acting tricks.

Chapter Eight

STEVE WASN'T BY ANY STRETCH an all-work kind of guy, despite his growing career and the pressures put on him by a resume that continued to stack up. He and Sally bought a house and they enjoyed turning it into their home, a place where they were making memories for their growing family. Every free moment of Steve's time was spent with Sally and Gaby. The couple would often work on the house while Gaby played nearby.

There were tall trees in the front yard in need of a considerable amount of thinning. Steve put his longstanding landscaping skills to use, for his own good this time. Sally described Steve as a true artist, and as he was in everything he did as an actor or a writer, he was a perfectionist.

He was this way with the trees, as well. Steve Ihnat didn't cut limbs; he laced the limbs. Sally explained, "That's when you go in and you don't just cut off branches, you cut off the little ones that aren't really adding to the beauty of the tree. They're kind of sucking from the bigger ones. Then you can see up and through the tree and make it more beautiful. Not so dense."

This particular day, Steve was in the tree, working non-stop for about an hour-and-a half. Sally was bringing him water, and then bringing him more water. When he finally came down to the ground, she was worried about him because "he did not look good at all. He was extremely flushed, and sweating profusely. It was a warm California day," she admitted, "but nonetheless his sweating was excessive. He sat down, I gave him cold water. I washed his face. He threw water on his face." Her concern, stewing in the back of her mind for quite some time, stayed with her and nagged at her. She didn't say anything to him but the sense that something might not be right with him never really left her.

That fall, Steve had his last appearance—though of course he didn't know it would be his last—on *The F.B.I.*, in a two-parter titled, "The Mastermind." The plot followed the pursuit of four men who robbed an amusement park, running off with $1,800,00. Along with Bradford Dillman, Scott Marlowe, and Steve, the fourth in the band of robbers was played by Steve's friend, Clu Gulager. Clu was the vicious killer of the bunch.

As Clu spoke of this show, he explained, "I starred in one of the hours and Ihnat starred in the other one. When I saw him, I would say, 'I was much better than you in your hour.' I don't know if he liked it or not. It was supposed to be humorous. Actors are not known for being funny. We can't tell jokes. We don't know what a joke is. We pretend and play like we do but we don't. We can't tell humorous anecdotes." Steve and Clu enjoyed playing off each other, and Steve was known by his friends to have a healthy sense of humor.

It was about this time Steve and Sally learned she was pregnant. They were beyond thrilled to learn they would become parents together, and immediately began planning for the addition to their family. While Steve was still, at this point, taking on television roles, his main focus almost

Steve in *Sweet Sweet Rachel* with Stephanie Powers, Chris Robinson, and Pat Hingle

completely changed. He was delighted his role of "Daddy Steve" was expanding.

A few TV shows, and a made-for-TV movie, *Sweet Sweet Rachel*—where he played a psychiatrist—finished up his 1971 credits. As a married man, he would soon have the responsibility of not just one but two children to raise. He had been in the entertainment business in Hollywood almost fifteen years, and was very familiar with how everything worked behind the scenes of television and film. He knew he must stay highly visible to ensure a decent paycheck continued to come his way.

He was confident enough in his skills to know he was in no danger of Tinseltown losing interest in him. He could always get work, just about whenever he wanted it. In fact, work came looking for him. He was certain he knew what parts would get him ahead in his career, and what would have him just skating along for many more years to come. Guest-starring on other actor's TV shows was a route always available to him for the foreseeable future but that wasn't the road Steve Ihnat wanted to take anymore. He could make a good living well into old age as one of those actors who became known as supporting this-or-that star, a back-up on every-and-any primetime television show on the air.

But Steve didn't want that, and continuing with the status quo wasn't in his playbook. He knew he needed to wisely plan any future moves if he was going to make changes. With his frustration growing more intense over the direction in which his career was currently headed—successful well into the future as a background, career character actor always skating big star status—Steve decided now was the time for a drastic move.

As Sally's belly grew larger, Steve recognized how the baby inside her would forever change the life they, and Gaby, lived, yet he still felt it was time to step out on the edge of his comfortable existence. *Do Not Throw Cushions Into the Ring* was completed. He was ready to show it to the world and had to get busy on promotion. That movie would be the catalyst to a different direction in life for him and his family.

Securing interviews was easy. He had a big enough name in the industry that the press "took his call" right away, and when it was discovered he made the movie, not just acted in it, this was definitely a worthy news story. "It's about an actor who has everything," he told a reporter in one of his early interviews, "all the material and professional proof of success. But he really doesn't want all the glamor and the money. In order to sustain it, he has to become a whore, creatively." Steve used all the right words to pack the punch.

Steve had made friends with some of the best known players in Hollywood over the years. He was a quick study and learned his craft well. Writing and directing were natural for him in his move up the Hollywood ladder. He had no problem getting the appointments needed, and was able to show his film to select individuals. *Do Not Throw Cushions Into the Ring* received promising initial commentary, proving to him he was ready to move forward and take the next steps. He continued to accept TV guest roles and movie work during this part of the process.

In 1970, Steve started working on Canadian distribution options for *Do Not Throw Cushions Into The Ring* on a trip home to visit with his family for Christmas. He arranged a special private screening at the Hyland Theatre to be held the morning after Christmas. Family, of course, was there, as were a few specially selected press people. Steve was close with local entertainment columnist, Ed Hocura, who always covered Steve's comings and goings, and who remained good to him in the press through the years.

About that screening Ed wrote in his column a few days later, "For a guy who has attended dozens of private screenings over the year, I must confess that the audience reaction to Steve Ihnat's one-man production made all the others pale in comparison. Call it a partisan audience, the fact remains that they responded to it with the kind of enthusiasm I had never experienced before."

Steve lined up a number of interviews during that trip, did lunch with any number of reporters and connections, and worked a small but defined promotions circle. He was interviewed by the *Toronto Star, Toronto Telegram*, and the *Hamilton Spectator*, and was heard on the radio with Betty Kennedy of the CFRB. Even local television, with the *Elwood Glover Show*, had him on their roster. Just before he left for Canada, he turned down another guest appearance on *Mannix* on United States television to keep this press trip going. He would've had to leave early to make the job, and the publicity he could get while working the Canadian circuit for *Cushions* was more important to him than the lost acting fee, or any additional TV credit added to his resume. Sally supported his decision.

Upon his return to Los Angeles, he continued television work when it came his way though, by his own design, such roles weren't as frequent since he was focusing his talents elsewhere. He wasn't one to turn down the paycheck, however, especially now that the paycheck financed not only his family needs but also his intent to enhance his industry profile.

Around Thanksgiving, Steve showed up as the lead guest star on a show which ultimately became known as *Men At Law* after changes were made to the script's premise. When it first came out, however, it was called *Storefront Lawyers*, as the story of three young, idealistic attorneys recently out of law school, of course near the top of their class. Any one of them could have their pick of the crop of high-visibility law firms across the country but they chose to devote their considerable talents to "relevant" law—"problems of the poor, the non-white and the disenfranchised."

Ed Hocura, *Hamilton Spectator* columnist, and supporter of Steve's work

The show starred Robert Foxworth, who went on to become well-known as an actor on the 1980s television show, *Falcon Crest*, as well as a director, and the widower of Elizabeth Montgomery. His cohorts in legal fairness for *Men At Law* were Sheila Larken and David Arkin.

In the episode, "The Pastures of Hell," (1970) Steve played Reverend Neil Dana, a white ghetto minister accused of kidnapping a militant black leader's son. Damning evidence piled up in the case against the reverend and he went to the lawyers for help. An unusual role for Steve yet he was believable and sincere in the part.

Steve filmed what should have been a big series opportunity for him in late 1971. A script which started out in October of 1969 was titled *The Pursuer*. Written by Bruce Geller for CBS, it began life as a series pilot. The last revision came a month or so later and by then the name was changed to *Hunter*. Indeed, the hunt was on for a star, and at the top of the list was Steve Ihnat.

He enjoyed this part, playing a race car driver, and became hooked on the sport by the time filming completed. He stated, "I'm ready for the checkered flag." Continuing on animatedly to a reporter, he said, "I play a government agent who's been unknowingly programmed to kill a fellow agent who, like me, is an amateur race driver." Yet again, Steve Ihnat was cast as another "government agent" with devious intentions.

The production shot scenes at Riverside Raceway for four days. The course was known to be a fairly dangerous one, used repeatedly in television and movies for its realism. Steve, never before having driven profes-

Steve in *Hunter*, with inset of John Vernon

sionally, started out slow, following behind a stunt driver. "…of course, I had to drive one of the cars." As he became comfortable behind the wheel, going around the curves and the long, downhill back straight-away, he was given more freedom to build up speed.

He explained, "There I was, lying practically flat, a must in the tiny cockpit, and before I knew it, I was doing 200 on the straight-away. I couldn't get over it when I slowed down—slowed down!—to 160." What happened next made him seriously consider his own mortality. "I'd been going around the track getting used to it, then one of the regular drivers took over. On his first lap, one of the brakes froze and he hit a wall at about 100 m.p.h." A scary memory. "The driver was only out of action for a few days but I get shaky thinking about what I missed."

Somewhere between the start of filming and in the protracted year *Hunter* took to complete, it was decided the project was too expensive to produce as a regular series. The entire idea, as such, was scrapped. Steve, as quick as he was handed his own series, now found himself out of a starring vehicle. In his own words, "So one year I was in and one year, I was out."

Yet in true Hollywood style, nothing was necessarily ever totally dead and buried. *Hunter* was resurrected and turned into a made-for-TV movie. There was, however, an unexplained change in casting. After the story was re-worked, John Vernon was brought in as the star, and Steve was made the co-star.

Interesting to note that Vernon was also a Canadian actor of similar background to Steve's, within a few years of Steve's age, and a comparable family history. There must have been something between the two men tipping the scales in John Vernon's favor, though what that was will never be known. Once more, Steve Ihnat was "thisclose" to becoming a household name on television, with his own starring vehicle, only to have the opportunity snatched from underneath him had *Hunter* made the grade on television. As it turned out, the opportunity did nothing for either man.

One evening not long after, Steve and Sally prepared to attend a party at Dory and Andre Previn's home. She was oh-so pregnant, standing inside their walk-in closet while getting dressed after her shower. Steve walked by the door and she looked up to see him laughing as he stared at her. His eyes were smiling warmly. She thought he was laughing at her and her huge belly.

"What are you laughing at?!" she exclaimed.

"I'm not laughing at you," he replied softly. "I'm just loving you, I'm just loving you, I'm just loving you...."

Their sweet exchange set the tone for their evening. They laughed, touched, having such a good time, as they always did. One of the guests at the party was Elizabeth Ashley who was then married to George Peppard. Sally remembered how Elizabeth was acting "wild," turning up the music and announcing to everyone, as if they didn't already know, that they were listening to "Dory's latest album." She kept the music outrageously loud, refusing to take it down a few notches as she flitted around the room, keeping right on Dory's heels every minute.

Sally, love of Steve's life and mother of his soon-to-be-born child

Finally, Steve tired of Elizabeth's antics. He wasn't angry; he was simply over her playacting and running around as Dory's shadow. Everyone else also appeared to be peeved but no one would say anything. Steve was never bothered with voicing his opinion. He'd never had that problem; he had a way about him.

In a mischievous, booming voice, he asked, "Does anybody have any Sinatra?"

This was pure Steve. Sally couldn't help herself. She started laughing so hard she left the room. Others broke into giggles right after her. Clearly, her husband was one who spoke his thoughts with the presence of mind to formulate what he would say before the words came out of his mouth. The party lightened up and Elizabeth calmed down.

Frank Converse came to Los Angeles during this same period for some work, and he and Steve met for coffee one day in Studio City. Frank thought it was amazing Steve "had these cans of film in the back of his car like he was peddling it [*Cushions*] around Hollywood," which is exactly what he was doing.

Frank was fascinated by Steve's tenacity. "I'll tell you what struck me about him. The fact that he was… the intensity with which he was pursuing a career as a director." Steve was pioneering a new way to use a camera lens and he showed it to Frank, explaining the process. "He found what was relatively new; a zoom lens. I'm going to say it was a 500 mm. He shot a demo of how to use this…. He was interviewing himself. It's really a cliché now since so many people have used it, maybe chiefly Steve McQueen in *Bullett*. But then, how you could use it to bring up objects, say a car from deep in the background into to the foreground, and Steve, he mastered this. I think he did this with money out of his own pocket. He got people interested in this. I think he networked the people he'd worked for."

The amazement was evident in Frank's voice. "I don't know how to explain it. I was sort of in awe of the gumption he had. I would say to myself, 'I wish I had that.' I would have somewhere to go from acting. Sometimes when you work in TV or movies, acting seems sort of like a dead end, especially if you don't reach a big level. As far as I'm concerned, I've always been happy with acting because it was a good living and it staked me for my life."

Frank was clear that he was happy and satisfied with where his professional world took him. He built a solid stage career, the sort of life he hoped for when he started out. Yet he always admired Steve Ihnat for his remarkable ability to identify what he wanted, and go after it without ever looking back or worrying over what-might-have-been.

* * *

It was winter in Los Angeles. The weather was comfortable yet Steve packed his bags and went north, leaving the mild temperatures for a colder climate. He'd accepted a role in a production for the Canadian Broadcasting Corporation (CBC), their television vehicle. The shooting locations would be in and around Toronto and Brampton in the thick of winter.

The producer, Ron Weyman, sought out Steve to return to his native Canada to play a "sensitive shop steward in the midst of an increasingly

Steve in a volatile scene from *Strike!*

bitter and violent strike in a small one-industry town." Steve's character was supposed to be a heavier man than Steve was at that point in his life. The director, Peter "PC" Carter, said, "He had the strange ability to put on weight very quickly. We said we needed a rather stocky figure and he showed up 40 pounds heavier."

Yet Sally indicated Steve did not bulk up for the role. She steadfastly has stated he was no heavier when he arrived in Canada than when he left home; he had not gained even a few pounds, intentionally or otherwise. She said he did indeed have an unusual talent, though, one where he could make himself appear as the role needed him to appear, and he employed this ability as required, putting himself inside the character's physical and emotional nuances.

The script was written by Grahame Woods, "a newbie freelance writer," as he called himself. He started writing in 1968 while working as a cinematographer for the CBC. By the time he wrote *Strike!* he went out on his own and offered them the script. They bought it and produced it as a one-hour television drama. The production, a "daring, punchy and raw" story, as Mr. Woods described it, opened their 1972 season. It created a controversy in its time because the story told of an "increasingly bitter and violent strike in a small, one-industry town."

Steve's character saw his hometown torn apart by the strife amidst a strike he initially supported, and even encouraged. He found himself part of the tension, with his own family crumbling in front of him. This caused him personal turmoil with his wife and daughter because without work, he could no longer support his family.

In the midst of the town's ever-growing environment of bad behavior, Steve's character encouraged the split between the haves and the have-nots by working for the strike's big boss. He was singled out as a driver, always sent to pick up and deliver the big guy's girlfriend to the small town for extracurricular activity. In the midst of this sidebar storyline, his childhood friend was murdered as he tried to cross a picket line. Steve's character finally decided something must be done and he changed sides, leading a back-to-work movement.

The girlfriend was expertly played by beautiful Linda Goranson, an experienced actress who has since worked on both sides of the North American television camera, as well as on stages across Canada. She called Steve a "wonderful" and "lovely" man. Their characters had bittersweet, heartfelt conversations about life in general, and how they lived in their small-town situations.

Steve Ihnat, left, and Sean McCann in Strike.

Steve as his opinions change in *Strike!*

From the writing of the script, to the direction of the action, beginning to end, to the acting, the entire production received excellent marks all around. Yet it was considered incendiary because of its subject matter and many thought it would cause a serious ruckus with the Canadian labor industry. One reporter wrote the film was "bound to get the CBC in labor's bad books." Another review stated, "The ending is sure to infuriate labor."

And one other predicted *Strike!* was likely to have only one showing, one night on CBC, and exactly that happened. Called a "play" by the CBC, it launched that season's anthology drama series. Steve's effort received such high marks that whether it was seen once or one hundred times, his work was publicly considered by all who remarked on it as a home run.

Reporter Blaik Kirby wrote a long, glowing review of the entire production. He said of Steve's performance, "Ihnat has only one big, impassioned speech, to a union meeting. But it is with acting, not just words, that he moves us.... It may be the most real and moving show you'll see all season."

Another reviewer, Jack Miller, boldly proclaimed, ". . . oh, if anybody was ready for stardom, Ihnat was in this role." Miller, also, believed Steve "put on a lot of weight" but that "added realism to the character. Of all his work that we'd seen, this was the best. The script called for a delicate emotional balance and he delivered—strong, sensitive, restrained, perfectly paced."

Miller's glowing commentary on Steve's performance continued. "If it had been coming up on a U.S. network instead of a Canadian one, we'd figure him a sure bet for an Emmy nomination next spring.... Among the Canadians succeeding in Hollywood," Miller concluded, Steve Ihnat wasn't "one of our most famous but... certainly one of our best."

Grahame Woods commented on the network itself, and Steve's work. "The CBC was very progressive for the times," he said, "taking television dramas out of the studio and shooting them on actual locations—a challenge for actors and crew but providing a realism that studio shooting often lacks. So Steve, most likely, would have found the shooting of *Strike!* stimulating and different.... Steve's role was... a very powerful performance supported by some fine actors of the day and director Peter Carter...."

Grahame Woods met Steve in person only once, "probably between takes or, fleetingly, on a lunch break.... In those days, writers stayed away from the set except for a courtesy visit. Also, in those days, once the script was finalized, it was stuck to." Yet Steve and his performance have remained in his mind over the years since as quality work. "*Strike!* was my 'launch' script and I was so fortunate to have Steve play the lead. I mean, how good could it get for that first venture?"

As always, whenever he had the chance to return home, Steve spent as much quality time as he could with family. He really loved the kids, and enjoyed having them around him. He felt that responsibility came along with his success, and had promised he would give back to his family by sending all his nieces and nephews to University.

On that particular trip, his niece, Brenda, remembered him gathering her and her little brother, Bradley Mordue, and plopping down in a soft chair. They also had another brother, Brent. With one child on either

Steve with his niece, Brenda, and nephew, Bradley; photo compliments Brenda Mordue-Humphries

side of his lap, he showed them what Brenda remembered as a "funny thermometer." A simple recollection which, years later, remained engrained in her adult mind of her even-then fatherly uncle.

That particular visit home carried a sadness, too. Steve's sister, Sue Makaj, had three children. A daughter, Bonnie, had died not long before of leukemia. There were two sons, Steve and Teddy. Another fan club gathering had been held while Steve was in town, and a lady by the name of Pat Robertson flew into Montreal to be there. The group enjoyed seeing him and when it was time for Pat to head home, Steve's uncle, Sue's husband, was tasked with taking her to the airport. Teddy wanted to go along and his dad reluctantly let him.

On the way back from the airport, a drunk, leaving a local Legion House, swerved to miss an Ontario police officer. When he accelerated past the policeman, he hit Teddy and his dad head-on, knocking their car into a ditch. It was a frigid cold day but the car blew up. Still, people stopped and helped to put the fire out.

They were hurt very bad. Teddy, who took a hard hit to his head, was given three hours to live

Steve with his niece, Brenda, and nephew, Brent; photo compliments Brenda Mordue-Humphries

once they got him to the hospital. Steve's brother-in-law was badly injured and hospitalized for quite some time. Teddy was in a coma for months and though he survived past the time the doctors allotted to him, he never enjoyed an independent life. He lived until he was fifty in a number of rehab facilities, forever after at the mercy of his parents to feed and clothe him, and handle each detail of his everyday existence.

This incident became a catalyst for Steve's nephew, Steve, to jump right into his uncle's footsteps. He was twelve when the accident occurred and it left a deep scar on him. "Our family was dealing with all these tragedies," Steve explained. "I became really unhappy." As the years went on, Steve was left much to his own devices as his parents poured all their time and energy into taking care of Teddy's considerable needs. Sally and Steve at one point even considered taking him into their home so he could have a fuller home life.

"The world was an unhappy place and I saw my uncle as... wow! His image, his life, became more poignant. I thought, in my young mind, if I could become like him, I could become happy. Movie stars had a great life. That's when, in those days, the seeds were planted and rooted.... I was close to him, felt very close to him." Steve Makaj decided then and there that he would follow in his Uncle Steve's footsteps and become an actor, a movie star. After all, he had been named after him.

Back in Los Angeles, Steve and Sally had a dinner date with friends on Christmas Eve 1971. They had gone shopping together a few weeks earlier. She caught sight of a beautiful coat in a store window and Steve urged her to try it on... just for fun. She knew they didn't have the money to make such a purchase but he wanted to see her in it. The price tag read $350. Far too much with all of their mounting expenses. A frivolous item which was not in their budget.

But they were having such a good time together, and she figured it would be a time-killer, so they went into the store. Smiling in anticipation, she asked to see this big curly fur collar coat which went down nearly to the ground. After the clerk brought

Steve's namesake nephew, Steve Makaj, an actor active on Canadian and U.S. TV

it to her, Sally wrapped it around herself, snuggled into it as best as she could, and started laughing. She could hardly get it around her ever-widening belly! Even so, the coat felt luxurious and it *was* lovely. She knew when she looked at Steve that he saw in her eyes how much she adored that fur coat. She didn't want to, but she took it off, thanked the saleswoman for showing it to them, and they left the store, going on their way. The coat was forgotten.

Or so she thought until Christmas Eve. As Steve opened the car door for her, as he always did, she saw a huge, stuffed-looking box with a big bow sitting on her side of the seat. She couldn't imagine what was inside and she just stared at it.

"Open it," Steve told her.

She did, bursting into tears when she saw what he bought for her. In reaction, as she put it, she "hugged and kissed him, and hugged and kissed him, and hugged and kissed him. Of course I said, 'You shouldn't have, we can't afford it right now.'"

Steve responded simply, "Just wear it, just wear it!" No matter that they lived in Los Angeles. And that she was pregnant and couldn't right now fit in the coat.

* * *

Barely a week later, just before the end of that year, Steve and Sally were in his big prized brown Bentley driving along Motor Avenue in Los Angeles, in the vicinity of Twentieth Century Fox studios. They were on their way to a dinner party, something they did often among their large circle of close friends. She was over halfway through her pregnancy, and the couple anticipated an exciting 1972 with the upcoming birth of their child. They couldn't wait for this addition to their family, and they believed things were really looking up for the Ihnats.

Suddenly, a car headed straight for them. Veering back and forth, erratic, fast, the driver seemingly had no intent, or no ability, to right his course. Steve had no time to make any correction or get out of the way, and by the time they hit, the collision was nearly head-on. Sally felt it was likely the massive size of the Bentley that saved their lives. What she remembered the most was the sound of metal hitting metal, and all she could recall Steve saying as the noise reverberated in her head was, "Oh shit!!"

Once he shook off the shock of the impact, Steve's only obvious concern was for her and their unborn baby. He wanted to make sure they were okay. She asked how he was, but he impatiently brushed off her concerns. He was fine, he said hurriedly. It seemed nothing less than a miracle they escaped from such a brutal crash with apparently little or no injuries.

Sally was horribly upset, she was dazed, but she seemed physically all right. She and Steve discovered the man who hit them was thoroughly drunk—that was probably what saved his life—and he passed out at the wheel. This was why he made no attempt to change his lane or get out of the way.

Once the police arrived and formalities were completed, and she and Steve declined medical attention, they called their dinner date and explained what happened. They asked if someone could pick them up and bring them to their house. No, they assured their friend, they didn't need to go home. They were fine. Yes, they still wanted to come to dinner. The friend showed up, drove them to the dinner party, and they found themselves to be the talk of the evening. Steve's car ended up in the shop for quite some time.

Chapter Nine

IN THE EARLIEST MONTHS OF 1972, while the weather in California was, as usual, sunny and warm, Steve returned to Canada, this time taking Sally with him. The weather there was anything but warm. Another reason he had left Canada—he found the climate so much nicer on the West Coast of the United States. This visit gave Sally a wonderful chance to make good use of her wonderful new fur coat.

Steve re-shot some scenes for his Canadian TV broadcast, *Strike!* As was the couple's habit, they crammed in as much visiting as possible with as many friends as they could fit in. Their schedule was hectic. Sally was very pregnant and everyone was thrilled to congratulate the happy couple. Guesses flew rampantly about the sex of their soon-to-be-born baby.

Brenda, Steve's niece, remembered her first meetings with Sally when Steve brought her home. "Aunt Sally was so glamorous and beautiful. I was starstruck and had a crush on her," she said. Sally gave Brenda her first lessons in girlish "womanhood," showing her how to apply makeup, put on fingernail polish, and all the things a young girl thought of when they dreamed of being a grown-up. "She always made all of us kids feel so loved."

Sally told of how the ritual was always the same when Steve entered his parent's home. His mother, dressed in one of her usual house dresses, her hose partly pulled and rolled up just beyond her knees, and wearing flat shoes, would run and hide in the closet. They would open the front door of the house and hear her, in her heavily-accented voice, as she keened, "Oh my boy, yoy, yoy, yoy...."

Steve dutifully went to the closet door, gently and slowly open it, and like the good son he was and always had been, he would coax her out. When they were ready to leave after each visit, she repeated this same ritual, but would sadly add, "Oh, you'll never come home again!"

Steve with his parents; photo compliments Ihnat Family Collection

During this visit, a party was put on at the family home, an old brick farmhouse on many acres. There was a big affair held each and every time Steve, the "big Hollywood star," returned home. Scores of friends, and the entire family—parents, siblings, aunts, uncles, nephews, cousins—congregated at the Ihnat farm. Steve found himself the center of attention, in particular with the children. The kids, as always, loved having him around to play with them and dote on them.

Pat Robertson, a member of the club who lived in Montreal, flew to Ontario for the party. Joan French, co-president of Steve's fan club, was there. So was her daughter, Sandy Brooks. Sandy told of one memory where, she stated unequivocally, "I think I fell in love!"

She explained that the children were "tearing around outside playing some kind of 'shoot 'em up' game," using their fingers as their guns. Sandy entered the house for a drink of water. Steve was sitting in the kitchen chatting with the adults.

"For some reason," she said, "I pointed my 'gun' at him and shot him. Well… he proceeded to die the most spectacular, dramatic death I had ever seen, finishing with falling to the floor and lying there dead. I was shocked, to say the least! I stood there for a few seconds, not knowing quite what to do… beginning to be a bit worried when he didn't move." Sandy was uncertain. Had she killed him? "Just as my lip started to quiver, he opened one eye and gave me a grin and a wink. He got some applause,

Steve with fan club executives—Dorothy Duncan, Irene Chapman, and Joan French—"Steve's Bunch"; photo compliments Joan French and Sandy Brooks

got to his feet and took a bow. I never forgot it.... I was probably about seven at the time. He was such a character!"

Many members of his local fan club attended these parties. Steve was grateful for their support and friendship, and loved to have them included. He always encouraged their participation in his visits back home. Joan French was talking with Steve, and she noted as he sat in his chair later on that day, he continually leaned over and rubbed the area right above his cowboy boot. He always wore cowboy boots. As Sally put it once, "Those were his shoes. In his head, those were his shoes."

"Is your leg hurting you, Steve?" she asked.

He lifted up the bottom hem of his pants leg to show her a large ugly red spot on his shin, the worst and nastiest bruise-like mark she had ever seen. In her words, it was "brightly-colored, translucent and horrible-looking." Joan knew he recently told Sally he didn't feel well, ever since the car accident.

"You really should see a doctor about that." Joan's words were stern, and she knew her look conveyed deep concern.

He sloughed off her words. "Doctors don't know anything," he replied in a take-no-prisoners tone of voice. His playful grin, however, was clearly intended to make light of the situation. In his non-confrontational way she knew he was, there and then, ending any discussion on the subject of his health.

One evening during that visit, Steve and Sally went to an old friend's home for dinner. Steve sat to Sally's left. The meal was over, and everyone was talking and laughing and having a wonderful time. Before this evening, she had never met any of these people but they were Steve's friends from years back, and she felt comfortable with them. Everyone accepted her as his beloved wife, and the evening was going along without a hitch.

All of a sudden Steve's face blanched an eerie greyish white. Sally explained, "I don't know if you've ever seen anyone when they're fainting but all the muscles let go. We don't know that we hold our face all the time in a certain way but all the muscles let go."

Steve slumped over his plate. He was out cold. No warning and for no known reason. Sally yelled, "Get his head down; get his head down!" Someone helped her get his head between his knees and, in that position, he slowly came back to consciousness. She and someone else pulled him away from the table in his chair. "Call a doctor!" She was scared. Frantic.

Steve foggily shushed her. He didn't want to be seen by a doctor, he adamantly told her and his host. He was fine, he said, just tired from all

Wayne Grajeda with his sister, Sally; photo compliments Wayne Grajeda

the activity going on. Everything would be okay after a proper rest. Sally, against her better judgement, allowed her husband to be the boss. He always had such a take-charge way about him, and he had taken charge once again.

That nagging sense of something not right with her husband's health returned to knock hard on her brain but she could not convince him he needed attention. No doctor came to the scene that night, and they returned to Steve's family home; he seemed fine during the rest of the trip. Life continued on. As usual.

Once he and Sally got back home to Los Angeles, Steve did not take a breather. He began immediately to make plans to go to the Cannes Film Festival in France. He got busy with plane and hotel reservations, securing preliminary connections, and making a secondary plan for a trip to see his brother-in-law in Germany, Wayne Grajeda, on the tail end of his trip before returning to the United States. It was Steve's intent to nail down solid distribution for *Do Not Throw Cushions Into The Ring*.

He and Wayne would, as Wayne put it, "have one of those bonding experiences that people share for a lifetime, in this case exploring the environs of Berlin together." He had been away from California for nearly a year and a half and planned to take Steve on a tour of the city, visiting the Wall and Checkpoint Charlie, one of the required American military posts for crossing into Russian occupied East Berlin, as well as other important landmarks.

Wayne was a musician and played many Berlin clubs. He intended to introduce Steve to "many of the denizens of the city's legendary nights. Cold War Berlin was an exciting, unique 'island' city, 100 miles inside Russian occupied East Germany. There were spies, artists, musicians, all manner of political parties, students, terrorist groups, armies (Russian, East Germen, French, British and American), transvestites… you name it."

Such an experience had the potential to add all sorts of material to Steve's repertoire for future performances. As Wayne aptly described it, "The city was a veritable stew of interesting characters an actor could file away in his memory to draw upon given the right script."

Wayne's musical abilities played heavily into the musical score for *Cushions*. His song, "Rising To The Bottom," according to him inspired to some degree by Hermann Hesses' book *Siddhartha* and "about a man's search for self-discovery," told of how expected happiness didn't necessarily bring success.

He explained that Steve's appreciation of the song clearly indicated they "were thinking in similar ways. When I played the song for him it seemed a natural fit and I greatly appreciated it when Steve decided to use it." From there, Wayne explained, "Steve then brought in an arranger who did some fine orchestrated versions of our music. It was an optimistic time for us all."

Clu Gulager ran into Steve just a few weeks before Steve left. Clu entered a restaurant and found Steve having a meal. Alone. He stopped to chat for a few moments and it wasn't long before he felt a bit troubled over their chance meeting.

"The last time I saw Steve was at a beautiful Italian restaurant on Santa Monica Boulevard between Beverly Hills and Hollywood," Clu explained. "He was eating a plate of spaghetti with veal, I believe. He was preoccupied. He had something on his mind. I don't know what it was... but it seemed to me that when Steve looked at me with those soul-searching eyes, because they always looked straight through you.... Steve looked at me, looked up from eating, and I thought, 'Wow, something's going on here, something not so good.'"

Even after he'd left him, for a long time Clu couldn't shake the feeling that Steve, for some reason, felt troubled deep down in his soul. "When he looked up at me, it seemed that something was going on, something unpleasant, like a, 'Help me,' a groping look, and I didn't know what that was about." He hesitated before he spoke again. "I'm not sure everyone knows they're going to die but...."

* * *

On the 12th of April, 1972, a perfectly beautiful baby boy was born to Steve and Sally Grajeda Carter Ihnat. They named him Stefan Andrew—Stefan after Steve, and Andrew after Steve's father. A prouder, happier daddy could not have been found at that moment in time. He had never thought he would get married, and the idea he would produce a child was completely out of any vision he had of his future. Steve Ihnat made plans for his life a long time ago but never in those plans had he seen this sort of joy in his vision. He was over the moon.

Here he was now, with a tiny replica of himself and Sally combined, a child they made together. An absolute miracle. Stefan's birth was physically hard on Sally. Steve stood by helplessly, unable to make it any easier for her, unable to ensure she and their baby would get through the experience without trouble. He was a strong man, physically and emotionally. He was known to set his sights on what he wanted, figure out how to get it, and take care of the problems certain to come up along the way.

Yet in this situation, as his beloved wife was in labor to produce their child, there was not a single thing he could do to make it better for her. There was nothing he could do to ensure she would come out on the other side safe and unscathed, and their baby would arrive squalling at the world as all healthy babies did. He and Sally had different blood types—his was "A," and hers wasn't compatible, which did cause issues during the delivery.

When he was allowed in to see them, he cradled Sally with his arm lovingly around her. His head was bent over her. He knew the doctors had been worried. She was ill, still thoroughly exhausted, and needed a good

Steve with his newborn son, Stefan, and daughter, Gaby;
photo compliments Ihnat Family Collection

amount of time to get her strength back. When he finally picked up his head and looked at her, Sally had his thick, wet tears on her arm. Strong, manly Steve was crying in overwhelmed relief. His wife and son would be okay. He couldn't hold back that emotion. This time, he was not acting.

* * *

Later that month, the day before Steve left for Cannes, he had a serious talk with Gaby's birth dad, Don. Sally remembered the conversation in great detail, even years later. Steve told Don that upon his return, he "would like to adopt Gaby. When I get back, can we talk about it?" Don readily agreed. This discussion was intended to pave the way for the process needed for Steve to legally adopt Gaby. He wanted her to carry the name of Ihnat into the future. She already lived with him as if he were her father, and he and Sally knew she loved him in that way. The four of them—he, Gaby, Stefan, and Sally—were already a family in every sense but name. Sally and Steve were eager to rectify the issue.

About this same time, David Carradine prepared to do a biker story, *You and Me*, written by Robert Henderson. His producing partner, Skip

Sherwood, originally wanted Steve to direct the film. This was a small independent work, and could have been a nice feather in Steve's moviemaking cap. His appeal to Sherwood was likely his ability to work with small budgets and get the most out of the meager amount of money available. Carradine and Steve worked together five years earlier when they played brothers in an episode of *Cimarron Strip*. This would have been another positive point. Steve would not have been a stranger to the film's star.

The production's promotional ace in the hole was the promise of Barbara Hershey as the female lead. She was pregnant with Carradine's child and though they would have to shoot her scenes early to get her in before she started to show, financing based on her in the cast was secured, even though it was only a paltry $60,000. Besides Hershey, the movie starred not only David Carradine but also his brothers, Keith and Robert.

Steve's scheduled trip to Cannes precluded his taking the job, however, and ultimately, Carradine, in one of his earliest efforts to do so, ended up directing the film himself. Steve was set to get on the plane for Cannes about the time work on the film was to start. There was no way he would change his mind. *Do Not Throw Cushions Into The Ring* was all-important to him and he was determined to make it a success.

* * *

Steve took that trip to Cannes. The Film Festival began on the fourth of May. He arrived the day before, late in the day, and proceeded to his hotel, the Villa Palma on La Croisette. The hotel, like many of the others, looked out on the beach. The scene was an idyllic one but Steve wasn't there for fun. He chose small, more "homey" accommodations, rather than one of the larger, glitzy places. He was cognizant of his budget, and he didn't need to be right in the middle of the action to achieve his goals. He could go where he needed to go, and return to his hotel, and his bed, for sleep only.

He went on this venture alone. All his preparations were made down to the last detail ahead of time. It wasn't until the next day that he would really begin to get his feet wet, figuring out the lay of the land and how he would proceed in getting his movie seen by the Powers That Be. There was so much work to do. He was a one-man power show. No assistants. Not only did he already plan everything, but he was personally lugging the film around the city in its large, heavy round tin canister. He'd need time to recover from the physical strain once he got back home but while he was there, he would do what he needed to do and damn the physical toil it might take on him.

By the end of the next day, after a good night's rest, he managed to nail down a screening with the Marché Du Film. This was the meeting spot for film professionals from all over the world, those wanting to buy, and those wanting to sell, film rights, or find co-producers, or backing, or simply to network with other film professionals. It was the "place to be" for someone peddling a movie, and Steve was there.

This was a Friday, and his screening was scheduled for Sunday. He purchased an ad in a film magazine, to run for two days. The ad cost $210, a sizeable amount, but he felt he had to do it. Even though he had already forked out one hundred dollars for the screening fee, he needed the added exposure the ad would bring him and his movie. As he put it in a letter he wrote to Sally that evening, "It's the only way to get things done—let's hope."

Sunday dawned, and Steve awoke, eager and ready to take on the day. This day would be an important one. He jotted off a quick note to Sally, telling her he'd met Charles Champlin, the *Los Angeles Times* film critic. Even before they'd come upon each other in person, Champlin recently proved to be a friendly advocate for Steve's work in a few of his columns. The two men had a drink together at the Majestic Hotel, a favorite place to stay for celebrities who came to the Festival. He and Charlie, as he came to know Champlin, got along immediately, and Steve told her Charlie would attend the screening. Steve signed off this letter with, "I love you I love you I love you."

Champlin said later Steve was "a versatile and gifted actor who was beginning to move into writing and directing.... He'd come to Cannes to see what he could do with *Do Not Throw Cushions Into The Ring*, his strong, skillful, and unsparingly honest film about an actor re-evaluating his whole life."

Steve also met a producer's representative from New York who planned to attend that same screening. Steve was hopeful this might lead to something. "It just may be the way to go," he wrote to his wife. "The market place here is a rat race. Lots of porn and junk. That seems to be the stuff most people deal in. The official entries of course are a different story altogether."

He had taken a walk the evening after he arrived to think and process everything going on. Since the beginning of their relationship, Sally often wrote love notes to him

Charles Champlin

and hid them in places where he would find them. She said, "I would put them in his pockets, in his shoes, in his socks, in his shirt pockets, his jackets, wherever."

This evening, an attractive young woman came up to him and propositioned him in French as he walked the Cannes strip. She said something equivalent to, "Hi, Sailor." Sally explained how Steve could become real shy in awkward situations. In a letter he had written and she received, sadly, about six months after he passed away, he mentioned this encounter.

"I put my hands in my pockets and shuffled a bit and felt a piece of paper and it said, 'Don't forget. If any of those women come up to you, you just tell them no.'" Steve did just that after reading the love note from his wife. He wrote in his "letter from the grave" that he told the other woman he had "the most beautiful woman in the world at home waiting" for him.

Steve in his glory with *Do Not Throw Cushions Into The Ring*; photo compliments Ihnat Family Collection

Steve worked Cannes from morning until late in the evening every day he was there. He did not waste a single minute of his time. He wanted so bad to be home with his wife, newborn son, and daughter. *Do Not Throw Cushions Into The Ring* was his passion project, true, but his family had taken on a meaning deeper than anything he had ever experienced. He told himself he was working so hard for them, for their future together, and this helped him keep plodding along.

Yet he was tired. So very tired. His body started to feel as if it could give out at any moment. In his letters, he mentioned to Sally more than once he was becoming sensitive to the effects of the non-stop activity.

On Wednesday, the 10th of May, Steve decided it was finally time for a good rest. He needed one. He had to do it. He allowed himself a few appointments that morning but then he put all his paperwork away—except for his letter-writing paper—and walked to the beach. He began writing to his bunch, as he always did, "My Darlings, all three...."

He informed them he was taking time to relax for the first time since his arrival in Cannes. He would quit worrying about business. At least for a little while. His words told his truth. He was clearly lonesome. "It's really miserable here without you and I miss you. I'll be happy to get home. I'd leave tomorrow if it wasn't for the 14 day air ticket and the fact that I am still accomplish[ing] things," he wrote.

The next part of his letter, "the longest letter I've written in my life," was clearly meant only for Sally. "This place is one grande whore house—wheeler dealers with porno and hustling producers." Referencing the hooker who approached him earlier in the week, "You have nothing to worry about in the girl department. There aren't any. They are all hookers. I've actually been propositioned twice at $100.00 per each." Mirroring the words he'd already told her when they had a similar conversation on the phone a few days before, he continued, "I just laugh and tell 'em I have a beautiful lady, thank you. I really do love you my darling. Actually (if it's any consolation) it's things like this that reiterate how special you are. In the world and especially to me."

He also wrote a letter to Gaby as he sat in the warm French sunshine, sand around him everywhere and people romping in the surf nearby. He was ever conscious of her as only a young child, yet he wanted her to feel as if she were an active part of the family experience between her mommy and him. To make certain she knew he was thinking of her as well as of her mother, Steve carefully printed a personal note from him to their daughter. It read:

Dear Gaby: I just want to say that I love you and miss you very much. I miss you and mommy and little brother and Bootsie. I will be home with you quite soon now. Then we will have a wrestle. Love from Daddy XXX

The outside of the envelope he addressed to "Miss Gaby Ihnat," put the required postage on it, their home address, and made sure it went out in the mail along with his letter to Sally.

With no way of knowing it, Steve would not be home "quite soon now," not as he expected to be, not as his family expected him to be. These letters were to be the last direct, living interactions Steve Ihnat would ever have with his cherished family.

Chapter Ten

ON MAY 12, 1972, SALLY AWOKE, feeling a smile automatically come over her face. It was her thirtieth birthday. Her beautiful new child, Stefan slept like the angel baby Steve and she knew him to be. He was in his crib nearby, and it was something of a birthday for him, too. He was exactly one month old today.

She yawned and stretched. It was time to wake Gaby and get her ready for pre-school. The sooner Gaby could get to school, the sooner she would be back home again. They would hear from Daddy Steve that afternoon. As a baby gift after Stefan's birth, she and Steve received a Super 8 camera from a friend, and had already used it many times to take family movies. In only one month's time, they'd amassed a decent-sized collection of wonderful memories of the four of them romping around. Sally had since added to the collection by rolling the film as Steve got on the plane, waving goodbye to his family, when he left for Cannes.

She and Gaby planned to record every facet of his return. Sally kept these sweet memories and their excited plans with her throughout her morning. She held close the happy thought that she would see Steve again soon, and the new movies they would take together would be only the first of many of their new happy brood. Steve was planning to adopt Gaby very soon. He loved the girl as if she were his biological daughter, and he wanted them all to be connected, family in name as well as in spirit.

Sally's day went by as normal as any birthday can. Turning thirty years old was a big deal. A friend offered to pick Gaby up after school and bring her home. Two more friends, Maritza Norman and her husband, Phil, stopped by around four o'clock, supposedly to deliver a birthday gift but that was only part of the plan. Their secret intent was to prepare Sally for a big surprise party later on. Maritza had a thick accent; she was Sally's only friend who was French born and raised.

She, Gaby, Maritza, and Phil clowned around as they awaited Steve's call. Sally pretended she was making an old-time movie, acting out a scene where Steve just phoned her. She portrayed a young woman hopelessly in love, patting her heart with her right hand as if to indicate it was fluttering uncontrollably. This was a silent production, or it was supposed to be, but the four of them laughed so hard, Sally found it impossible to stay quiet and pretend to be in character. No matter, they were having fun and passing the time. There would be no Academy Awards given out this day.

Gaby had followed her mother's direction and gone into her room to change into her play clothes when the phone finally rang for real. Sally jumped for the receiver, so hoping it was Steve, expecting it to be him. On the other end, the long distance operator inquired of her if Monsieur Bootsie Ihnat was home.

Bootsie was their dog, a black poodle mix. They always used him as the central character for the signal she and Steve worked out for each phone call he made to her from overseas. Sally was expected to respond, "No, Bootsie isn't in right now." She and Steve would each hang up, and Steve could then call back directly, knowing she was at home and there wouldn't be a charge for a missed call. It was cheaper that way.

This time, though, she paused for barely a moment. Something unexpectedly nagged at her, she didn't know what, just an uncomfortable sensation which came over her, telling her to accept the call. She hastily spoke to the operator, "Please put him through. I accept the charges."

"I will advise my caller."

The line went silent and when the operator returned to Sally, she sounded confused. "I am sorry, m'am, but my party has cancelled the call." That was it, and she hung up. No explanation given.

Sally sat there a moment, stunned, shaking her head. Steve would never just hang up on her. He wouldn't "cancel" a call to her. He wouldn't

Sally with Bootsie; photo compliments
Ihnat Family Collection

do that. He would know how worried she would be. Never would he hang up on her. Unless....

Sally didn't like what went through her head after that "unless" thought. She dialed the long distance operator back and asked to be put through to an international operator. Giving the phone number in France, she said she wanted to be connected to the Villa Palma hotel in Cannes, Steve's hotel.

"Maritza," Sally turned to her friend, "would you handle this until we get Steve on the line?" Since French was her mother tongue, Maritza could easily explain to Sally what was said on the line while Sally nursed Stefan. He was overdue... and so was her body.

The American long distance operator put through a call to the French operator but could not make the connection. Eventually, she told Maritza, "I have called using several lines and, believe it or not, France isn't answering. I'll let you listen in." Maritza turned and explained to Sally that the other end kept ringing and ringing. No response. The operator could hardly believe it; neither could Sally or Maritza. The operator continued to try, rerouting the call through a number of different trunk lines, making the effort for the next hour and forty-five minutes.

Finally, an international operator picked up and they were connected to the hotel desk, with Maritza asking for Steve Ihnat in French.

"Oh yes, Madame, could... could you hold a moment?" The clerk's voice, responding in thickly accented French, was hurried and shaky. Maritza explained to Sally that the phone receiver had been unceremoniously dropped onto a hard surface. A good amount of time went by before she again heard anything on the other end. She related, finally, that she could hear voices speaking low, in rushed, agitated, muffled tones. She couldn't tell what they were saying, though, she told Sally. Then, abruptly, that line disconnected. Went dead. The hotel hung up on her. Without explanation.

Maritza relayed all this to Sally, bit by bit, keeping her apprised of everything. Sally continued to nurse Stefan and tried, unsuccessfully, to keep her cool. Her little girl, Gaby, for the most part unaware of the sudden drama going on nearby, had returned to the room with them and was playing on the floor with Bootsie. Sally could tell, though, that Gaby, too, felt the discomfort growing around her. It was obvious the edgy mood that came upon them without warning affected her, as well.

Maritza tried to put another call through with the help of first the American, and then the French, operator. This time it took twenty minutes to get the connection. A new voice at the hotel's front desk, sounding even more breathless than the first clerk sounded earlier, said, "Allo, Allo." Maritza whispered to Sally it clearly was as if the hotel was waiting for this return call.

Sally watched, now angry as well as worried, though she had no idea why she was angry, or even who she should be angry with. Steve? The people at the hotel? All of them? She didn't know what was going on in France at Steve's hotel. It was early morning there. Was he playing some crazy joke on her? Or was he.... ? No, Sally didn't want to think he'd gotten sick. During their last conversation he told her he wasn't feeling right. She wondered if he was forced to hang up because he had to run to the restroom, or some such.

Suddenly, she saw Maritza's entire body go rigid. Her friend turned her back to Sally, who watched as Maritza's shoulders slumped. She lowered her voice, and now spoke in a hushed but thickening whisper. Sally could still hear what she was saying but she couldn't understand a single word. When Maritza's tone changed again and became alarmingly loud, her raised inflections were blatantly shocking.

A few minutes into this oddly-changing conversation, Sally gasped when she heard Maritza rasp out one word as a harsh question, "Morte?!"

Sally had never spoken or understood French but she knew what that stark word meant. Maritza pivoted and, with a ragged breath, looked directly at her. Her face was blanched. "There is a doctor on the phone and he wants to speak to you, Sally." Maritza's efforts not to sob were unsuccessful, and Sally, in that one moment, completely broke down. She didn't need to understand French to know what she was about to hear.

Tears rolled over her cheeks. She couldn't breathe right. Grasping for the phone, she managed a weak, jagged greeting. A man's voice responded in broken English, "Madame," she heard, "I am sorry to tell you but your husband has died."

Just like that. No preamble. No, "This is what happened." Sally could not believe her ears. No. No! Clearly they had the wrong person and she adamantly told him so. This man who died, he could not be her husband. Steve was only thirty-seven years old and he was in excellent health! So strong, broad. Healthy. He had a physical just before he left on his trip.

"No, Madame, it is him. He had a heart attack." But what about the wrong room number? Did they have the wrong room number? She thought about her husband before he'd left her as this insane conversation continued in her ear.

The doctor's English was difficult to understand as he mumbled something about Steve found in the tub, something about a hot bath. Something about having been called earlier because he hadn't felt well. Something about giving him nitroglycerin tablets, and telling him he'd return later if he didn't feel better soon. Something about... about... Steve was dead before the doctor could see him again....

Steve was so big and strong, she kept saying to herself. *He'd had a full work-up for the insurance company on his new film*, she thought, *and was deemed to be in perfect health.*

"No, not my Steve," she mumbled. "No. Are you sure you're talking about Steve Ihnat?"

"Yes, Madame. I am so sorry."

There were no more words. She wanted to know why this man called himself a doctor. This was a man who supposedly knew enough to give her husband a heart medication but hadn't immediately sent him to the hospital. She could not speak, though. Her own heart was in her throat.

Steve on 1st wedding anniversary; photo compliments Ihnat Family Collection

Her own heart was irretrievably broken. She was shivering uncontrollably, and Maritza quickly took the receiver from her and hung up.

Sally couldn't process this news. This… could… not… be… happening. *We are very much in love*, she sobbed. *He is my prince charming, the sexiest, most handsome, kindest, most gentle, funny—so funny!—and dedicated, creative, talented man in the world. We just got married and bought this lovely perfect home. We just had our beautiful baby boy. Steve would adopt Gaby when he returned from France. He is going to adopt Gaby! He is committed to our family. We are a family! I've never belonged to anyone else. I adore him and feel so loved by him, so deeply loved….*

Gaby watched her mom as all this went on. She had no idea what was happening as the tragedy unfolded in its earliest hours, one which would prove to also affect her deeply. All she could figure out was that something was wrong, very bad wrong, something about Daddy Steve. No one would tell her anything, though. Earlier, as they tried to get their phone call to work, they said he had a stomach ache but would be fine soon. Now, she was sure it had to be a really bad stomach ache for her mom to cry so hard and to look like she would never again be able to smile.

She was just a little girl, only six years old, but she was smart, and she knew Daddy Steve was in big trouble. She could see it on her mom's face, she could see it in the tear's falling down her red cheeks. She saw it in Maritza's big, scared eyes, who looked at her as if she didn't know what any of them would do next, and how could they take care of her and a little baby, and whatever this problem was. She could see it when Mr. Phil looked at her, too.

Gaby was so frightened, and she began ripping at the striped long shag rug she sat on, ripping at it and ripping at it, taking out her frustration and fear of the unknown on the only thing at hand. She didn't know who it was who came to her, or when it happened, but at some point someone picked her up and held her tightly to console her.

But… why?

* * *

Several people came by that afternoon, and long after the sky turned dark. The house was filled with worried and grieving friends and family, all wanting to comfort and help Sally but not knowing what they could do for her. There was no fixing this heartbreak. Everyone was at a shocked loss. This was so totally unexpected.

Steve with Gaby; photo compliments Ihnat Family Collection

Through her mental fog, Sally learned there was to have been a big surprise birthday party for her that night at a famous nightclub on Santa Monica Boulevard. The evening should have been a big bright night of grand celebration. Instead, it became countless dark hours of interminable mourning.

Someone cancelled the party plans. Someone else corralled all the people who, as they heard the news of Steve's passing, came by to support her, not knowing how to fit in but wanting to help in any way they could. The overwhelming mass of caring individuals, however, just became too much for Sally to handle. She was in such a state of shock she was beyond being able to function.

In the midst of it all, the children still needed tending. Gaby was finally told the truth, in as few, and simple and understandable words as possible. The little girl was distraught. As for the baby, Sally's breast milk suddenly and totally dried up and she could not nurse Stefan. Her emotional state overtook her bodily functions, and her heart now ran the show.

Before Steve left for France, he had tried to think of everything his wife and family might need while he was away. He was a take-charge sort of man and didn't want his wife in want while he was so far from her and unable to fix things for her. One of his solutions was to hire a wonderful nanny to help with the children. The woman's primary task was to support Sally, and to do whatever was necessary to make his wife's life easier with these two young kids while she was alone with them.

The African American woman he brought in was by nature quiet and gentle. She was also steely strong, physically and emotionally. Steve could have never known what an excellent choice he'd made when he brought her into his house, or how well she would take care of his family in his place.

The nanny saw that baby Stefan was getting hungrier and hungrier and Sally was literally unable on her own to do what she needed to do. Without missing a beat the woman immediately took charge, barking orders in every direction.

Someone needed to get to the market right then and there, and buy beer. Beer, of all things! Steve Lodge, Steve's friend and writing partner, rushed out the door to take on the task without asking a single question. When he returned in short order, the nanny silently took the six-pack from him, popped open a can and in a no-nonsense tone ordered Sally to drink every drop without questioning her, assuring her that her milk would come in if she drank enough.

Sally hated beer but she was so exhausted and unaware of reality she blindly followed directions. To everyone's surprise, except for the nanny who knew it would work, the beer did the trick. After several downed cans of the sudsy brew and a few hours later, a totally inebriated Sally felt the milk begin to engorge her breasts. She nursed Steve's infant child with tears still streaming down her flushed face. Baby Stefan finally fell asleep, now fully satiated, and the nanny gently took him from his mother and put him to bed.

Then it was Sally's turn. Someone else took charge of her. Somehow, she got through that evening. She didn't remember sleeping at all, though she was fuzzily aware several people stayed at the house to closely watch over her. The next day, and all of the following days, were a blur. Sally had to make a horrible phone call to her brother to let him know Steve would not take that trip to see him in Berlin. The call was excruciatingly painful. Another long-distance operator-assisted effort, bringing to mind the far-too-recent efforts to get Steve on the phone.

Wayne explained how it happened. "The night before the morning of Steve's highly anticipated arrival I was playing at a small club named, amazingly, the Steve Club. It was about midnight and I was on stage when, between songs, the bartender yelled out that I had to telephone the U.S. as soon as I got off stage.... I was expecting to meet Steve about ten hours later.... I would pick him up at Tempelhof Airport, the legendary landing strip for the Berlin Airlift after WW2...." He went to a friend's apartment and made the call to Sally to learn the devastating news. He immediately began planning his trip to Los Angeles to be with his sister.

Sally was never sure she was able to truly feel the sadness which was there with her right under the surface at every turn. Time for grieving was put on the back burner until everything related to Steve's death could be handled and put away in its proper place. Sally, as his widow, was filled with the horror of taking care of each detail surrounding the totally un-real reality of Steve being gone. Forever.

Of course his family was informed, and they were inconsolable. They came to California as soon as they could get there, and Steve Lodge was once again given an important task, that of picking them up at the airport. He made himself available to do anything and everything he could to help Sally during this difficult time.

When he picked up the family, Steve's mother didn't speak except to tell Steve Lodge, in heavily-accented English, to, "take me to the child!" She wanted to see her grandson, and she meant immediately.

Upon their arrival at the house, his mother followed some other friends to where a baby was sleeping in a back bedroom. Mrs. Ihnat dropped to her knees and, as Sally explained, began to keen in an Old World fashion. She was so distraught she had no idea who else might be around her but she really didn't appear to care.

"Oh my son... oh my baby boy...." She wailed and she prayed for some time, still on her knees. This was her way of mourning the loss of her dearly-beloved son. Steve meant everything

Steve with Steve Lodge; photo compliments Steve Lodge

to her. He was her Golden Boy. Baby Stefan was her one remaining link to Steve.

She was certain her sweet Steve was murdered. Nothing or no one could dissuade her of this idea. She had no basis, or any proof, but Mrs. Ihnat was certain someone had somehow killed her son. She told Sally this more than once.

Things got more bizarre with each passing hour, and every day thereafter. Few people outside of Steve's immediate circle of family and friends yet knew he had passed away. The news filtered out slowly within the industry, person by person by person. The one individual who did the greatest to tell the world that the most famous unknown name in acting in Hollywood was dead proved to be his friend and fellow actor, Ed Asner.

Ed learned of Steve's death from Sally. He and his wife, Nancy, were neighbors. Their son, Matt, often played with Gaby. At one point, Matt had given Gaby a pair of cowboy boots he had outgrown. She wore them constantly because she loved to copy her Daddy Steve, who always wore cowboy boots. Sally said he considered them to be his daily shoes.

Two days after Ed learned of Steve's passing, the Emmy Awards went on in all its usual pomp and circumstance in Hollywood at the Pantages Theater, hosted by Johnny Carson. Evening temperatures were comfortable, allowing nominees and wannabes to parade in abandon along the red carpet dressed in enough rented, borrowed and advertised glitzy finery to blind a distant planet. Some of these people did not have a clue who Steve Ihnat had been. Yet many more not only knew him, they had worked with him, and others had worked for him.

A good number of them were bona fide friends. Others admired him. Just about everyone who recognized his named respected him for his work in an industry known to chew up talented professionals, and spit them out like yesterday's tasteless dinner.

So many people there appreciated Steve Ihnat, had laughed with him, broken bread with him, and knew he was on his way to becoming an integral part of the national and international entertainment industry. Steve was familiar and well-known to his peers. His face became increasingly more sought-after to people who saw him often in the last ten or so years on both the small and big screens. Those who were seen on the screen, and those who put the faces on the screens to be seen, these were the individuals in the audience in Hollywood that evening.

In theory, it may not have seemed odd that Ed Asner brought up Steve's name when he won the Emmy for Outstanding Performance by an

Actor in a Supporting Role in a Comedy, for his portrayal of Lou Grant on The Mary Tyler Moore Show. What was odd, however, was how he did so.

With his official light, funny, airy speech nearly completed, Asner looked down at the podium and stalled a second or two before speaking again, his voice sobering, suddenly deep with emotion he seemed to try unsuccessfully to mask.

He went through his thank you list, finishing in a sad voice with, "And, I'd like to thank publicly, and belatedly, Steve Ihnat, who died a few days ago, a fine actor, fine filmmaker, fine friend. I shall miss him...." A few seconds after these words trailed off, he began speaking again. He regained a smile to his tone and face as he offered his last sincere vote of gratitude to Mary Tyler Moore.

Ed Asner moved on quickly, giving the audience little time to digest what he said about Steve. Many would later admit to being stunned. Others would say they weren't certain they heard him correctly. Steve Ihnat was dead? Friends of Sally who were there said a collective gasp rippled throughout the crowd. Some of them cried. The news was so shocking and bewildering, and delivered in the midst of what otherwise was a happy moment.

The television viewing audience was just as incredulous. Fans across the country who were happily enjoying the Emmy Awards show found themselves staring at their TVs in horror. Sally was also watching and hadn't expected the news to be announced that way. She didn't know Ed Asner would tell the world her husband was dead.

She took a few moments to process what Ed did, and then realized he had done her a big favor. Sally didn't have possession of Steve's address book. She believed he may have taken it to France with him and nothing had been returned to her yet. She didn't know how to get hold of his friends and co-workers to give them the news. Now, she didn't have to. Ed had done that for her.

Steve was never a publicity hound. He was better known within the entertainment world by the quality of his work, or the public that waited each week to see him on television, than by any press which followed him around. He never really worked to "brand" himself in the eyes of viewers; his art was what was important to him. He felt his work branded him, and nothing more was necessary.

In publicly telling the world of Steve's passing, Ed Asner in some ways unintentionally became Steve Ihnat's posthumous publicity person, a role no one had ever officially held during Steve's lifetime. He'd had a manager and an attorney, but not a press person. For weeks afterward, letters came into network offices pleading for information. Some were addressed to the shows Steve had acted in most often but in a twist, most were addressed to Ed Asner, for Steve Ihnat. People begged him to say they had heard him wrong. He hadn't said Steve was dead, had they? They wanted to be told something else, just about anything else.

What Ed did say about Steve in later articles was deeply personal about his friend. "Steve had a large ego but coupled with it were love and generosity. I experienced all of them and can only express amazement and envy at the response the news of his death evoked.... The intensity of love and sorrow I've witnessed by his friends and fans is remarkable.... I hope it will suffice to say that I considered him a great actor, filmmaker, and friend."

All the letters Ed fielded in Steve's name were ultimately forwarded to Sally. From Rose in Rome, NY: "I just watched you receive the Emmy Award... you mentioned... your dear friend, Steve Ihnat, had died a few days ago. Mr. Asner, I'm still in shock! I didn't know Mr. Ihnat personally but he has been my very favorite actor since I first saw him act in a television series *Outer Limits* about nine years ago. I've never been able to find out anything about him in any magazine, etc. Oh, he was so very good in any part and I think I've seen just about everything he's done. I just wait for the *TV Guide* magazine to come out every week so I can check through to see if 'Steve is on this week.' I will miss him so much and, although I didn't know him, believe me, I will grieve, too. I've tried every way to get a picture of him and find out all the things a woman wants to know about her favorite movie or TV star. His birth date, height, weight, color of hair and eyes, is he married, does he have children, etc., etc., and in Mr. Ihnat's case, the origin of his last name. It has puzzled me for years. Is it German, Slavic, Russian? I've never heard the name before...."

From Arlene in Cincinnati: "... I was truly shocked at your statement of Steve Ihnat's death. I have admired this man for years.... Whenever we saw he was to be in a series episode, we always watched it. I had often wanted to write to him, but I didn't have the faintest idea of where to write. Now I'm sorry that I didn't at least try...."

From Melissa in Orient, Iowa: "... I was watching the Emmy Awards last week.... [Steve Ihnat] was such a fine actor. Any role that he portrayed, he did it so convincingly. His face was so expressive. Although I am a 32 year old farm wife and mother of two young children, I wrote him a fan letter last fall. Each week I scanned the television section to see if his name was listed. I knew anything he was in would be worth seeing. But now there are only memories...."

There were so many letters from Steve's fans that Sally received them for a long time afterward. She couldn't read them all but they were kept. She was touched to learn that her husband meant so much to so many people who appreciated the man, as well as his work. Steve would have been honored to know he achieved his goal every time he went in front of the camera.

Sally received condolences from people who knew Steve professionally and just couldn't believe he was gone. Addie Gould, who had represented him for a time, was "so very shocked and saddened." In later years, she said of him, "He was a good actor and very bright." Ms. Gould "loved being around him," found him entertaining, and a very good storyteller.

Actor Frank Converse said of his friend, "I don't know who the Steve Ihnats of today are. It's too bad that his life was cut short. He was this gifted guy who died before he could realize his real potential... but I think he literally did realize it. That was a tragedy. His talent had found another avenue and it was cut off. Steve did a Clint Eastwood on us on a lower scale. He didn't wait to become a big name, he just did it. He just pulled the rabbit out of the hat. It wasn't sleight of hand. He knew what he was doing."

A letter Frank wrote to Sally when he heard of Steve's death clearly represented what many in the entertainment industry felt about the loss of such a man. ". . . he was an ideal of mine. It may not seem much in the ordinary profession to triumph over the obstacles of institutionalized methods, and insecurities, but in ours to believe it is to do well... if a man does it on his own terms as well as those of his imagination. I miss him particularly as I don't have too many acquaintances pursuing such individuality and because I was truly shocked to find such a man existed. He took care of business."

Morgan Brittany, as a fully aware child actress, worked with Steve on *The Outer Limits*. She spoke of him as an actor and a person, bringing full circle the remembrance of someone so many knew from afar, and so few knew close-up. "I don't think Steve was the kind of guy who would have gone the publicity route. He didn't strike me as that kind of an actor, the sort that wanted the spotlight. He didn't hit me that way. I can tell. I can tell the kind of people I'm working with, who crave the attention, who crave the fame. I know that just in the way they act. He wasn't like that at all. Given the opportunity, I think he would've been one of the memorable actors of all time."

Chapter Eleven

IT TOOK WEEKS TO GET THE CIRCUMSTANCES surrounding Steve's death organized, and to put him to rest. After the initial shock began to settle in, the conditions of his passing hit Sally hard and she began to speculate over the odd details. Many family and friends held some of the same concerns. Years later, Steve's nephew, Steve Makaj, said, "We as a family felt bad. We wondered if somebody did something to him."

Steve's death seemed downright peculiar, at best. A man in his mid-thirties who by official medical records was listed in excellent health, who was strong and solid and led a physically-active lifestyle, usually didn't simply drop dead of a sudden heart attack, which was the official reason given as the cause. Could there have been some other reason?

There had been no autopsy. Sally was told in the initial phone call that the symptoms Steve presented to the physician caused the doctor to ultimately rule his death as a heart attack. Cardiac arrest.

She was told after-the-fact by Bob Gurney, an American who befriended Steve in Cannes, that the doctor suddenly left his practice. When Steve, whom the physician called the "young man," died so suddenly, that same doctor felt guilty because he wasn't able to, or hadn't tried to, save him. Sally wasn't aware which reason may have been correct. And why would a doctor leave a man alone he suspected of having a heart attack? This would have been, at the very least, negligent.

To Sally's knowledge, there was no police investigation. She was not once contacted by any officials, French or American or Canadian. Despite the fact that Steve was a Canadian citizen born in Czechoslovakia, living in the United States on a work Visa and visiting France on a travel Visa, it appeared on the surface that no Embassy became involved in any way after his death.

165

If there had been governmental involvement, Sally had lost sight of it in all the confusion. Steve's manager and attorney, Myron "Mike" Emery, managed his business affairs, as well as some of his personal concerns. Any official interactions must have been through Emery's office without the widow's consent or involvement. Sally has since said she wasn't sure if she trusted Mike Emery and, more so, his business partner. Steve had but she held reservations about them.

Her concern over Emery's business practices may have best been exemplified when his partner visited Sally right after Steve died. The unnamed partner, along with his wife, came to see Sally, ostensibly to commiserate over her loss and give his condolences. As she indicated, "He stayed for three hours and charged me $1300 for that condolence!"

She was now a widow, a single mother with two children to support on her own. Gaby was a little girl, and Stefan only a month old, still breastfeeding. Her husband was dead under strange conditions and no one of any consequence seemed to be the least bit interested. Just the tasks of everyday life would be difficult for her to accomplish in the coming months, nonetheless the idea of trying to launch an investigation of her own into his passing away in a foreign country. Finances were now a big concern which grew bigger by the day. To mount an official investigation from the United States seemed an impossible effort to her. She could not afford it. She didn't have the time to take away from her children. And frankly, she simply did not have the emotional strength anymore.

The insurance company for *The Honkers*, however, Steve's last officially-completed film, did have the time and the money, and they did do an investigation. They weren't about to shell out $100,000 to Sally if Steve committed suicide, or if his death resulted from other unnatural conditions, without looking into the cause. Their relatively cursory look-see satisfied the bean counters and she received the money which, while helpful, hardly lasted long enough to cover all the mounting expenses.

There were people, other than his mother, who honestly thought Steve might have been murdered. This was an off-the-wall idea. Who would want to murder Steve Ihnat? Why would anyone want to murder Steve Ihnat? Yet the state of affairs surrounding his death were so jarring and inconsistent that such a possibility now seemed not so outlandish.

Steve was fine one second, dead the next. He made an expected phone call, as happy as ever, and hung up in a mysterious rush the next minute. The story went that a doctor reportedly saw him alive and unwell and thought he appeared to have already had a heart attack, prescribed him nitroglycerin tablets, and simply told him to go to bed and rest. Hours later, the doctor told Steve's wife her husband was dead from a heart attack.

That same doctor was the one who gave the official cause listed on Steve Ihnat's death certificate, a document which certified his case forever, yet did so without solid, irrevocable proof. Without an autopsy done on the body of a man, a stranger to the doctor, who passed away alone in a foreign country, there is little to corroborate this story.

The doctor reportedly, of his own account, was spooked into giving up his practice abruptly after Steve's death because of his lack of follow-up. And to top this all off, belongings disappeared from Steve's room when a list of his things was made to send home to Sally. No investigation was done as to who may have taken these items—money, an expensive Red Cross pocketknife, a director's film loop, and other personal pieces.

So why would Steve Ihnat have been murdered? Who would have motive to do him in? He had no known enemies. There was one certainty, however. Steve died as the result of one of two situations, or possibly a combination of both, the least nefarious being inept medical attention which, in today's world would be considered criminally-negligent.

The most eccentric prospect considered was that someone did kill him. There would have been any number of plausible scenarios, from simple robbery to complicated international espionage. As was known, Steve Ihnat was a Canadian born in Czechoslovakia who lived in the United States and died in France. The circumstances of his heritage, as well as his acting background, covered all the bases.

He had become quite successful in recent years, and was known in the industry to be someone to keep an eye on. Steve Ihnat was going places. His visibility had risen greatly around the world. Actors, directors and producers commended him for his generosity to his cohorts. His ability to transform himself into all sorts of personalities and nationalities was applauded, and in demand.

His moviemaking was receiving a good amount of positive buzz, particularly from his directorial debut of *The Honkers*. *Do Not Throw Cushions Into the Ring* seemed headed into distribution, more toward arthouse theater circles rather than general circulation. It likely would not have grossed large amounts of money even had it reached a hefty population of moviegoers. The film, still, was an accurate and creative representation of what Steve could do, and would have brought him more work, and a good amount of continued attention from the industry and the viewing public.

What happened to *Do Not Throw Cushions Into The Ring*?

Steve with his parents and Douglass Jackson at wedding reception;
photo compliments Ihnat Family Collection

A friend, Douglass Jackson, agreed to take the script to the office of the Writers Guild of America (WGA) for Steve just prior to his trip to Cannes. Steve was rushing around to get things finished before he left, and Doug, thoughtfully everyone believed, offered his help, willing to do anything he could for Steve. Doug was something of a Guy Friday, and Steve asked him to have the script registered in his name at the WGA.

Instead, somewhere between leaving Steve's presence and before his arrival at the Guild office, Jackson managed to artfully remove Steve's name as the writer, and add his own in its place. This duplicity wasn't discovered until after Steve's death, and just prior to his funeral. When she learned of what Doug did after the WGA called her to inform her of the suspicious circumstances surrounding the script's registration, Sally asked friends to have him physically barred from the funeral.

She was furious, but even more, she was disappointed and saddened. Doug had been Steve's friend for years. He became her friend, and a shoulder to cry on in the recent weeks. He had, in fact, known Steve longer than she had. Doug came to the United States from Canada, seemingly on Steve's heels, and most believed he knew Steve there.

Just before the funeral, Doug took Sally to lunch, acting as a dear, dear man, empathizing with her over their loss. How could he turn on Steve this way? Why? What did Doug expect to gain from such an underhanded move? How did he think he could get away with the lie even if it got by the WGA? Sally would never know the answer to those questions. Doug disappeared and has never been heard from since.

However, *Do Not Throw Cushions Into The Ring* did somehow manage to find a public audience. As Charles Champlin put it in a letter to a fan of Steve's, "there is more interest in the film now he is dead than when he was alive."

Steve's friend in Cannes, Bob Gurney, arranged a well-attended memorial showing which received great acclaim. Bob was an American filmmaker and director who'd gone to Cannes years earlier to promote his work. He loved the area so much he moved his family there for a while and opened an international school, branching out of the film business.

Bob also did a bit of informal agenting for the film for Sally from his home in Cannes, sending information around the world on the film, on Steve, and on his untimely passing, to producers and distribution companies and executives he knew in the movie business. He was successful in gaining attention. One letter to her explained his results.

"Before you get this letter," Bob wrote, "you may have been contacted by a Marty Bochner of Astral Films of Toronto, Canada. He has said that he definitely wants *Cushions* and will pay a cash advance of some kind for it against a distribution deal. He has also said he would see that [Don] Rugoff in New York sees the film and thinks he may go for it."

Bob continued with his advice on how to proceed when Sally heard from Mr. Bochner. He felt it would be best for her to "take him seriously" and deal with him "for Canada—but at this time for Canada only. He offered Steve a deal whereby he would prepare the campaign—the press book—trailer etc. He thinks he understands the film and this might work out."

This commentary suggested Marty Bochner spoke with Steve in Cannes and arranged, in discussion if not in writing, some sort of potential deal regarding *Do Not Throw Cushions Into The Ring*. Bob Gurney went so far as to end his letter with his assurance of more effort on this angle. "I am going to have Charlie Cooper and Marty Bochner, contact of Astral, contact Al Golbert directly and see what happens." He seemed to feel there was serious possibility of having Steve's film find an audience.

If this Marty Bochner moved forward with any sort of deal, and put the film into the hands of Don Rugoff, there may have been all sorts of opportunities for *Do Not Throw Cushions Into The Ring* to find a large-scale audience. Had Steve passed on the information to Mike Emery? If so, what happened next? Sally never heard of the results and Steve never had a chance to explain.

Rugoff was a well-known champion of the art cinema genre, and dedicated his career to making certain such films received a lot of attention. In the 1960s, he was established as a premier exhibitor of "art-house product." He built his business on "an identity based on its otherness…." This description fit Steve's film to near perfection. *Do Not Throw Cushions Into The Ring* was highly personal, a deeply introspective story which relied on the viewer's mind to move them through the plot, rather than physical on-screen action.

So where had these potential "deals" gone while Steve was still alive? Was there a handshake and a pat on the back between him and Bochner, with an intention to later turn that into a contracted sealed deal? Research has not yet answered that question. Rugoff has passed away, and Bochner hasn't been located despite effort to do so. Mike Emery is also deceased.

What has been uncovered, however, is a curious development. Somehow, the movie ended up in at least a few years of television distribution. Sally said she never signed anything authorizing such action, and has never once received royalty payments. Yet numerous television guide notations have been found throughout the early and mid-1980s advertising *Do Not Throw Cushions Into The Ring* on United States TV, usually shown in the evening, and most often in the southern states and California.

9:00 ⑪

DO NOT THROW CUSHIONS INTO THE RING
(1978) Steve Ihnat, Edward Asner. An ambitious actor achieves the American dream of "success" and then reveals the story of his broken marriage, his alienated child, and his friends that have turned into enemies.

1980 newspaper ad for *Do Not Throw Cushions Into The Ring* on TV, indicating the film was made in 1978—six years after Steve's death. How did this happen?

Douglass Jackson had access to the script. Mike Emery may have had access. Did either man ever have access to the film itself? There were only a few copies of the movie originally created. Steve had one with him in Cannes. That copy stayed in Cannes and Bob Gurney used it for promotion after Steve passed away. It has apparently since been lost, probably not well-labeled and gotten rid of when the Gurneys moved from France back to the United States years later.

Sally possessed a copy, kept in California and which remains in storage to this day. The only other known copy is in Canada in the family's possession. If there were so few available operational tins of the movie which could be used to professionally put it to use, how did it show up on TV some nearly-ten years after Steve's death? Who was the driver, or who were the drivers, behind this? Who profited from the distribution? In those days, there weren't ways to electronically transfer media from one method of operation to another without utilizing the actual work or a physical copy.

Yet another mystery surrounding the life, and death, of Steve Ihnat. So many unanswered questions which, it would seem, will never be answered.

* * *

Steve's funeral became another major point of contention after the circumstances surrounding his passing was settled, at least to most people's satisfaction. A ceremony meant to console and help the grieving process instead became a harrowing task, one which others seemed to want to argue about with Sally at every effort she made. The churches and priests to which she turned all refused to do a service the way she and, she was sure, Steve, would have wanted it done.

She tried to get a Catholic church involved by picking up the phone book and calling just about every one of them in the Los Angeles metropolitan area. Steve's mother and father were Russian Orthodox Catholic. Steve was baptized in the same faith but hadn't followed it in his adult years. Steve didn't consider himself a Catholic. As Sally said, "He was way more spiritual. He was very spiritual. He did not love the Catholic faith at all." Nonetheless, she wanted to honor his family by burying their son in the ways of their religion and she was determined to do so.

Finally, someone referred her to a Paulist priest who sympathized with Sally's feelings and beliefs. Just so happened this young priest had been an actor, and he said he would check with his superiors to see what he could do, and he would call her back as soon as possible. When he returned her phone call, just as he promised, he told her he jumped through quite a few hoops but was eventually given the go-ahead to perform the ceremony exactly as she wished. Sally stated she was "elated."

The parts of the ceremony upon which she was unwilling to compromise were indeed unique requests. She was fully aware they were but she stood her ground. The music from *Do Not Throw Cushions Into the Ring* was to be performed on tape by Sally's brother, Wayne Grajeda, who wrote the music with Steve's approval. She would not have, as she put it, some "dirge" played in its place. That would be totally unacceptable.

The funeral was to be scheduled in the evening so Steve's friends could be there after they got out of work at the studios. Their jobs weren't the sort that they could take the day off without any repercussions. She understood this, and she knew Steve would have, as well.

One of her last requests was very much out of the ordinary. She wanted Stefan baptized at the funeral. She staunchly did not believe in death, and she wanted the cycle of life to be glaringly evident, and have it celebrated in clear view of everyone, with the participation of all their family and friends. In her words, "I believe we change forms and move on to whatever our next lessons are, and that's indeed what Steve was doing. So I wanted to celebrate the life that he had blessed me with, which was Stefan."

Not only did Steve pass away on her thirtieth birthday, but that day marked one-month exactly since Stefan was born. Sally saw extreme significance in this. There was unconcealed meaning in the cycle of Steve's life, and his death. She said about her husband and Stefan's father, about his leaving the earth, "Electricity doesn't die. It just changes forms." She needed to have that message impressed upon all who knew Steve.

It seemed fitting that the priest chosen to represent him in death was a unique exemplification of religion in his own right. Father Bob Curtis was only a few years older than Steve. He had not set out to become a man of the cloth. He had been in the Air Force and, after returning home, studied acting at American Academy of Dramatic Arts in New York.

His stint as an actor, however, was short-lived and unsuccessful. His spiritual life weighed heavily on him and he chose to enter the priesthood. He never fully lost his flair for acting, or actors, however. He was grateful when his request to be assigned to a parish in Los Angeles was granted, and he was allowed to minister to a local acting community.

Father Curtis' empathy for the heart of a performer made him the perfect spiritual connection for Sally during this difficult time. He was in tune with her feelings and her needs. He was one of the few consumers of television entertainment who was unaware of Steve and his work prior to finding himself called on to represent him into eternity but, as he wrote to her later on, he felt Steve had "come alive" for him through Sally, and her and Steve's "beautiful man-child."

On top of all of the other trials which accompanied the ordeal, trying to get her beloved husband's body back to the United States was a nightmare for Sally. She was forced to cancel his finally-scheduled funeral three times as his space on prearranged flights was bumped unceremoniously, reportedly by the airlines. The whole thing was, Sally said, "unbelievably dramatic...."

As Steve's body continued to be held in France for the airline to return to Los Angeles, once, then twice, "they would bump him." That second time, Sally related, happened just moments before she left for the church to verify all the final arrangements on the day of the funeral. Everything was scheduled and arranged. Everyone was ready to go. When she received the phone call telling her Steve would not be coming home as scheduled, she was forced to cancel everything. Again. Guests had to be contacted and told not to come to the funeral home.

"Why, no idea. They'd just say they couldn't carry any more luggage... they made him sound like luggage. They made it such a terrible feeling." Sally was put through hell, and the disrespect shown to her husband as a human being was nothing less than callous. Someone's suitcases were considered more important. Sally had gone through so much already.

Finally, on the third try, she told everyone, invitees, the church, all involved, that "whether Steve shows up or not, we're going to do the service," just as if he were in attendance in living body. When the entire effort was completed, it took about three weeks to get Steve back to the States from France. No satisfactory explanations were ever given to Sally. No interventions from any officials of any sort were offered.

The lack of respect for human life was never accounted or apologized for by anyone at the funeral home in France, or within the French or American government, or the airline. If Mike Emery was in that mix, he never said anything to Sally.

She initially planned to have Steve cremated. Sally explained, "Funny but Steve I and had talked about it a few times. 'Well, if I die,' one of us said, 'I'd like to be cremated.' 'Yeah, me, too,' the other said. So, I had told his family that was what I was going to do when his body got home. They went nuts. His mother, bless her heart, she went ballistic. She thought he was going to live into eternity in ashes. He wouldn't have his body. She was very Old Country. She could speak English but it was broken. His dad, as well. He didn't speak any English. She was so broken up about the thought of Steve being cremated that I just said, you know what, Steve isn't here. He doesn't care. He's gone on. So I said, okay, I won't. I won't. I'll have him buried."

It turned out to be an expensive venture for a woman who was newly-widowed, newly-in-charge of every part of her financial situation, and dealing with the sudden and unexpected death of her husband. Sole support of two very young children as well as herself, she didn't know what money would come in next, where it would come from, and when it would get to her. The entire funeral cost $11,000, and was held at the Westwood Village Memorial Park Cemetery. Sally was immediately familiar with the establishment, and they knew of Steve since he had filmed there.

The family got to the church for the third attempt at a funeral on time, not knowing whether they would have a service with, or without, Steve. They were situating themselves in the chapel when Stefan began crying uncontrollably. Sally was still nursing him and hadn't lost the feeling of being in a state of shock over the rapid-fire events of the last days. She wore a dress a friend helped her buy just for the service. They'd run to the store a few days prior and picked up nearly the first thing they found. Just pulled something off the rack.

She remembered, "When I think about this dress, it was ridiculous…. I found this long, little dress… pin-dot fabric, little dots in it, dark navy blue. To the floor, zipped down the back. I didn't want to nurse in the church so I took Stefan into the bathroom. Somebody helped me and I covered the toilet seat with all kinds of paper. I sat down, unzipped the back of my dress, and pulled it down, nursing Stefan, and then I started to laugh, with tears in my eyes.

"I looked up and said to Steve, 'Are you getting a load of this?! I'm sitting on a toilet, nursing your son, at your funeral. This is bizarre! This is something you'd put in a film and nobody would believe you!'" Even in the midst of such a shocking tragedy, Sally found the humor. The act of sharing it with her beloved Steve, as if he were right there next to her, laughing with her, released the burden of her sorrow just a little bit. She literally felt him with her in that extremely personal situation.

The service was performed, finally, exactly as Sally requested, but she wasn't completely relieved until they left the church building and began on their way to the cemetery. There was still that nagging, one unknown factor. Would Steve be late for his own funeral?

"We never knew until, literally, the hearse rounded the corner and drove up to the front of the church," she explained, "whether Steve was going to be there or not because they didn't have cell phones then. I can still see that hearse drive right around that corner...." Her sigh of relief was heartfelt. Finally, Steve was home. This would happen. She, Gaby, and Stefan would be able to put their beloved to rest. He was, as the inscription on the cemetery plate read, their "darling husband and daddy," and, at last, he was brought back to them.

There were many, many people at the burial site. Friends from all areas of the industry, as well as other parts of Steve's and Sally's life came to pay their respects and give her their love and support. Connie Stevens was there, as was her brother, Chuck, also a close friend. After the ceremony, Chuck leaned over and put his hand on Steve's casket. "Goodbye," he whispered as he walked away.

Gary Clarke came with his wife. After the burial ceremony, his wife went on alone. He stood by himself on the lawn and he said he felt bereft. His friend, Steve Ihnat, a man like a brother to him for so many years, whom he'd known since he entered the crazy world of Hollywood, was gone. Forever. A man he'd lived with and with whom he shared so many of life's experiences, good and bad and fun and ugly, would no longer be there to tease him or laugh at his silly jokes, or even for him to argue with. This was not make-believe. This was not acting. Gary burst into tears. He could not move.

He felt he and Steve had unfinished business between them, and the emotions of hurt and some guilt tore at him amidst his sorrow. There was so much he still wanted to say to his friend, so much he wanted to share with him. Now, he would never be able to do so.

He stood there remembering some of the issues that separated him and Steve over the years. At first, not even marriage took away their closeness. The duo continued to pal around and enjoy each other's company for a few years after Gary said, "I do." When Gary married his first wife, Pat Woodell, Steve was in the wedding party. Pat had recently become popular as Bobbie Jo Bradley, one of three pretty, sweet, and squeaky-clean sisters on TV's *Petticoat Junction*. She was also a singer.

A few years afterward, he, Steve, and their friend, Basil "Brad" Bradbury, were at his place talking about a film they planned to write together. The three of them were always involved in some sort of new venture, and this time they were huddled around his kitchen table, discussing the project. There was little preamble after Steve and Brad walked in his door. They went right to work.

Thinking back, though, Gary realized later Steve seemed as if he may have had something else on his mind. Something that could have been troubling him, or really preoccupied his thoughts, at the very least, and put him in a dark mood.

Pat came into the kitchen and asked the three of them a question. Gary couldn't even remember the question anymore but he and Brad responded right away. For whatever reason, Steve did not. He wouldn't even raise his head and look at her. Pat asked again, this time pointedly speaking directly to Steve.

Gary remembered that though Steve hadn't replied, he had a "pissed" expression on his face. It was Steve's reaction that got Gary's attention, and he tore into Steve with a vengeance for what he considered to be a slight against his wife. Steve was rude to Pat, in his mind, and there was no call for that. Gary had no idea what was eating at him. Steve simply had never acted like that before but whatever had him so upset, Gary felt he didn't need to take it out on Pat. He abruptly told Steve to leave his house. Right then and there. Without a word, Steve got up and calmly walked out. The two men didn't speak again for about two years.

In hindsight, all these years later as he stood outside the church after Steve's funeral, Gary was certain Steve had something on his mind that day which hijacked his usual calm behavior. Something put Steve so out-of-sorts, something which turned a normally thoughtful and social man into a sullen and uncommunicative stranger. At least for that point in time. The behavior was so unlike the Steve he knew, and Gary was shocked into acting harshly.

Yet there was no way of knowing anymore what happened to start that chain of events. Nothing could ever answer that question now.

Gary's heart continued to take him back in time. He recalled coming home a few years later to find Steve once again in his kitchen, and this time, he was talking to Pat. Animatedly so. She and Steve were not only cordial, they were warm with each other, acting like the old friends they had always been. Steve treated Gary that day as if nothing ever happened between them and as if they hadn't been separated for some time.

Gary sat down and Steve let him know Gene Roddenberry came to him with a script for a new television series to be called *Police Story*. He wanted Steve to star in it, and of course Steve was excited. His own series! Gary could feel his anticipation. Finally, after working so hard for so many years for this very thing. Gene and Steve thought Gary would be great as the co-star, and Steve wanted to be the one to tell him. He personally went to Gary's home to offer him the part on behalf of Gene. Gary accepted, of course, and just that fast, their friendship resumed the feeling of its earlier closeness.

.... Gary's thoughts jolted to the present. Right then, a car came around the corner, slowing down and stopping near him. The door opened, and Sally got out. She walked up to him and without saying a word, they embraced tightly. Both cried, and cried. The wife and the old friend. They comforted each other for a long time. No words were said. No words needed to be said.

Once everything finally came together, the funeral was over, and Steve was put to rest, Sally was able to get home, to take a breather, and reflect on the events of the day. Later she remembered, with a heavy sigh of relief, "It was unusual but very appropriate for Steve."

Epilogue

STEVE DIED ALONE IN A HOTEL ROOM, in a foreign country. His death was officially listed as a heart attack. The following is believed to be the particulars about the events immediately leading up to his passing, as best as can be surmised from available facts. Whether or not the cause was actually a heart attack is questionable because, for unknown reasons, that autopsy was not performed. It took no less than three weeks to have him returned to his family in the United States for burial.

This creates one unquestionable fact—the ultimate truth will never be known. What details are obtainable have been pieced together in the most cohesive way possible utilizing what is currently known to have been Steve's potential health concerns, as well as his personal habits and schedule while in Cannes. So many scenarios are plausible concerning the reason behind his death. Some are logical, some maybe not likely, but all possible.

The facts of his life have been presented. The environment in which he lived as it was has been presented, as has been all other factors. In keeping with all the unknowns, the only option has been to let the reader make her own evaluation. It has been the author's honest intent to lay out every fair telling of Steve Ihnat's life, which includes the sad reality of his untimely and shadowy departure from this earth....

It is known that Steve placed the phone call to Sally through the international operator from his hotel room prior to his death, in the exact same way he called her a number of times since he arrived in France. He would have the operator put the call through, Sally would answer, and the operator would tell her Monsieur Steve Ihnat wanted to speak with Monsieur Boostsie Ihnat.

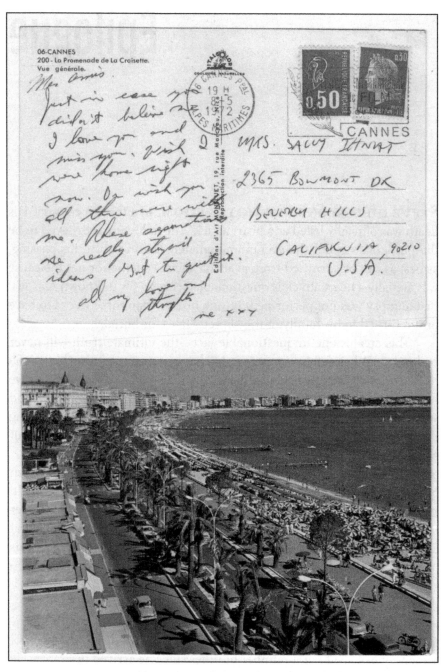

Postcards from Steve to Sally and kids from Cannes;
compliments Ihnat Family Collection

The operator had no idea Bootsie was a dog. Sally would, with a wide grin, tell the operator Bootsie was not there at that moment. The operator would return to him, informing him of Bootsie's absence; he would thank her and then hang up... after which he would call Sally back directly. Bootsie was, of course, quite a talented pet but hadn't yet figured out how to answer the phone.

It would seem logical to believe Steve felt okay when he placed his call that early morning in his usual fashion. No physical pain. A call from France to America took some amount of time to complete the full connection, however, and could have been more than enough time for circumstances to change in no more than an instant. Clearly, this time something did happen as he waited for Sally to respond on the other end.

Sally said he'd told her earlier, during another phone call, that his left arm, as well as his back, was hurting him. He lugged the heavy and awkward film tin all over town for days but that may not have been the only reason his arm and back hurt. He'd had intermittent issues over the years with his scoliosis. Too much walking, sitting, or standing, and carrying something heavy in the process, all this could have been a consideration.

Or... there may have been some other issue in the mix, something not obvious.

The operator put him on hold as she spoke with Sally to connect the call. What happened then is unknown. Could Steve have had an explosive sensation down his left arm? Did his chest start to hurt so bad he couldn't hang on? Might he have dropped the receiver? Maybe he felt as if he just could not go through with the call at this point. It is known that he was back on the line when the operator returned to him to connect the call. When she said his party was ready to speak with him, he told her he was disconnecting, and unceremoniously hung up without another word. This is what she told Sally.

Did he then call the hotel Front Desk to ask for a doctor? One account, unverified and coming from an unknown source, said he had done so. If he did, how long did it take for the physician to reach him? It's important to remember once Steve hung up on Sally, it took about two hours for her friend, Maritza, to place the call again, and for the call to be reconnected with the hotel's Front Desk. Two hours.

What exactly went on during that time is truly not known. One account indicates that Steve called the concierge and a doctor, a local pediatrician and family physician named Raymond Martinez, was summoned.

He was known to cater to the expatriates in the area, and saw hotel guests with health concerns.

According to that report, Steve must have managed to stumble to the door and open it. Dr. Martinez was approximately Steve's age. He probably did all the usual things a doctor would do when checking on a patient. Certainly Steve would have been able to tell from the way the doctor checked him out that there was something causing him to be worried about his new charge. Yet again, this is conjecture.

What the never-before-researched version of this story has related all these years is how the doctor did not tell Steve what he suspected was wrong. It has been recorded in the past, however, that at that moment he had strong suspicions. Instead, Dr. Martinez reportedly said something to Steve to the effect of, "I have some pills for you," and he gave him nitroglycerin tablets. "Take one of these now and put it under your tongue. Let it dissolve," he said, or something similar.

Would a family physician who usually made commonplace "house calls" carry nitroglycerin pills in his bag of tricks to see a new patient at a hotel? This is unknown but it might seem odd. Had Steve suggested to the Front Desk when he called to ask for a doctor that he felt he might be having heart trouble? Unknown. Had the hotel staff, in turn, suggested to Dr. Martinez that Steve might be in the throes of a heart attack and this is why he carried nitroglycerin with him? Again, this is not known. The hotel is no longer in business, and no staff members have been located.

It was reported that Dr. Martinez let Steve know he would return later to see how he was doing. If he wasn't feeling better, he would ensure Steve got to the hospital and they would run tests on him. He gave his patient the pills, and ordered him again to take another in a few hours if he thought he needed to do so.

The long-accepted story goes on that the doctor had a sense of what already happened to Steve, prior to his arrival to check on him, but he said nothing to Steve because he didn't want to worry him any more than he might already be. He was fairly certain Steve had a mild heart attack and this is what caused him to ask for a doctor. He seemed to show all the signs, though by the time Dr. Martinez got there, Steve looked as if he was stabilizing. This gave the doctor some confidence that Steve would be okay. Dr. Martinez must have let himself out of the room, and this would have left Steve, once again, alone. All by himself.

There is documented fact regarding Dr. Martinez and his practice. He was a family physician in Cannes and, now retired, he lives in the same place in which he lived and worked forty-five years ago. He was tracked down with the help of Doug Gurney, the son of Bob Gurney, the man who befriended Steve after Steve's arrival in Cannes.

Bob has since passed away but his son, Doug, shared information about the doctor and his father's friendship with Steve. He also happened to be the Gurney family physician. That Dr. Martinez took care of Bob's family, and he was the hotel's doctor-on-call is believed to have been no more than a coincidence in this small town.

Between the details Doug related and additional research by the author, Dr. Martinez was located and agreed to share his recollections of the time surrounding Steve's death. Dr. Martinez informed the author he was called to the hotel to attend to "Monsieur Ihnat." The doctor remembered the circumstances "very well," he indicated, stating he "came to the hotel after a call from the concierge." When he got there, his email read, "Mr. Ihnat was already dead [a] victim of a heart attack just after having a warm bath in his room!"

This definitive statement from the doctor differs starkly from the story that has been told for the last forty-five years since Steve's passing. It does, however, make some sense of a few discomforting details. Would a physician worth his license, a physician who thought a man who'd already experienced one heart attack, leave that man alone in a room with nothing more than a few pills, telling him only that he'd check back later?

Such treatment would be patent negligence, at best. Thoroughly unacceptable. In the United States, such behavior, then as well as now, would be cause for medical malpractice. If Steve suffered a heart attack prior to the doctor's arrival, assuming that was a correct diagnosis, and the doctor had taken Steve to a hospital immediately, he could potentially have been saved.

What the doctor's recent comments have not cleared up, however, was how anyone could know definitively that Steve had a heart attack, and if he did, how it was as a result of a "warm bath," or a shower. Again, if Steve was in his room alone when he died, all of these details could only have been assumptions. Nothing more.

So who actually made the initial assumption? If Dr. Martinez saw him prior to his death and presumed he had a heart attack, it is true that from his professional opinion, he was qualified to make such a medical assessment. Yet Steve was reportedly alive when Dr. Martinez left his room, and died later. His review of Steve's symptoms were cursory, and he didn't spend a lot of time with him based on everything which has been reported over the years.

And how did anyone know Steve had drawn a *hot* bath, or a shower? Was the water still hot when they got into his room and found him? If so, they must have reached him just after he died. Water in a tub does not stay at that temperature for a very long time.

There were maybe two hours between the time Steve got in the tub and the time he was found dead. The complete timeline is determined from the moment he hung up after he called Sally, until the moment the hotel manager entered his room and found him dead. For starters, there was a total of about two hours which elapsed between his call to Sally and her call back to the hotel. He was still alive then.

Another ninety minutes between her second call and that call's disconnection by the Front Desk. Was he still alive at that time? Unknown. Then maybe thirty minutes between placement of the third call and Sally hearing of Steve's death from the doctor. This constitutes the two-hour period in question.

Considering how long it would take a man in as great pain as Steve was reportedly in to undress, wait for a tub to fill with enough hot water to give him the required comfort for soaking—he was not a small man—and climb into that slippery tub in his ailing state, there would not be much more than an hour-and-a-half of those two hours left before Sally's last call to the hotel was received and she was informed of his death. Still, that's a considerable amount of time for a tub of water to stay "hot."

It's important to remember that during this unthinkably horrible time for Steve, Sally went through her own nightmare. Trying to get hold of her husband, with a sense of dread building in her heart moment by moment, she watched her friend do everything she could for her to connect with the hotel through the international telephone operator.

It was somewhere in here when Maritza finally reached the Front Desk. The phone was picked up, then brusquely dropped on a hard surface. Sally heard Maritza speak to someone in the office in French in hushed tones, and at that point the call was disconnected. No apology. No explanation. Not another word.

Why?

In the meantime, at his hotel, in his room, the official telling of Steve's story has been that he must have stumbled to the bathroom and turned on the tub water, and kept it running. Since he was alone, this has to be conjecture. He must have been fitful, likely unable to lie down or sit up or move around well enough to take himself out of his room. The pill he was given, if he had been given a pill, clearly offered him no relief. It makes sense to think he must have tried anything and everything he could to relieve his pain, and couldn't figure out what to do next. It is known that he took off his clothes because he was found naked.

From the way the story has been recorded, he managed to climb into the hottest water he could stand. In his agony-riddled mind, it would seem he thought the heat might make him feel better. Nothing made sense to him anymore. He had to get rid of the terrible ache in his chest. That was all he wanted. He needed to feel better. He had to feel better....

* * *

It is fact that somewhere about an hour or so later, the hotel manager broke into Steve Ihnat's room after desperately trying to get him to answer the insistent knocks on his door. This timing correlated with Sally's third attempt, through Maritza, to get hold of him by phone, and it is assumed that the concierge finally reported the situation to the hotel management. When the room was opened, Steve was not immediately found. When the manager heard bathwater running, he walked in the direction of the sound, calling over and over, "Monsieur Ihnat? Monsieur Ihnat?"

No answer. Just the droning sound of water.

When he steeled himself to look into the bathroom, Steve was in the tub, water running over his lifeless body. A question that has yet never been answered... was the water flooding the room? If it was running ever since Steve turned it on, surely it may have by this time overrun the tub.

There were never any answers to some important, curious questions. Was the drain stopped up, or open? Where was Steve positioned in the tub? Was he sitting up, or slumped to the side? Was his head above, or under, the water? How did anyone know he hadn't fallen into the water? Or been placed there? Or been pushed? Did anyone check for any marks?

If he'd gotten into the tub on his own steam, how do we know he didn't hit his head entering the tub? How does anyone know, for certain, that he got into the tub to make himself feel better because his arm and chest were hurting? There were no reports in Cannes of him mentioning such an ailment to anyone, or any ailments, for that matter.

After all, he was the only one in the room so what happened to him preceding his death was factually unknown. He *had* been the only one in that room, hadn't he?

The currently-accepted telling of Steve's story is all according to piecemeal supposition based upon different perspectives from the few people Sally has been able to rely on from her long distance vantage point. She was never once able to speak with an official of the French, American, or Canadian government. Never talked with any member of law enforcement from any of the governments. Never spoke with anyone in the French funeral home which embalmed Steve's body, the same one which arranged to have him sent back to the United States.

Mike Emery took care of the final details. He acted as the bridge between her, the distraught widow, and the complicated red tape surrounding his client's unexpected departure from this earth. Since he has also passed away, any insight he could have offered has been lost to time. Yet when everything was fluid, he gave no clarifications to his client. Sally was never the wiser as to anything Emery may have known about circumstances surrounding her husband's death. At the very least, he should have insisted on an autopsy.

One thing was certain, however, no matter how it actually happened. Steve Ihnat was dead. What truly happened to this young American actor, a man born in Czechoslovakia, raised as a Czechoslovakian citizen resident of Canada in his formative years, to become a resident of the United States as an adult? This actor who died in France? Steve Ihnat lived as a man who wore many faces, a complicated and mysterious man of many nationalities, and many voices.

He died as that same man.

Steve's grave marker

At times life deals a painful blow
That's hard to understand.
We try our best to comprehend
The ways of God and Man.

We lose our calm reserve
And think: On what can we rely?
We get confused and tearful
As we keep on asking, "Why?"

The "why" is so illusive
That we turn to what we trust—
The promise that the love of God
Will always nurture us.

No life is ever ended,
Whatever path is trod—
It's held intact forever
In the shelt'ring arms of God.

~ Marcella Krisel, 25 February 1976
Grandmother of Gabriel "Gabi" Michel Ihnat

Films & Television

FILM

1958: *Dragstrip Riot*... Dutch
1960: *Date Bait*... character unnamed
1963: *Strike Me Deadly*... Al
1964: *Passion Street, U.S.A.*... Dick Budman
1965: *Brainstorm*... Dr. Copeland, Intern (uncredited)
1966: *The Chase*... Archie Cloud
1967: *In Like Flint*... Carter
1967: *Countdown*... Ross Duellan
1967: *Police Story* (TV Movie)... Capt. James Paige
1967: *Hour of the Gun*... Andy Warshaw
1968: *Madigan*... Barney Benesch
1968: *Kona Coast*... Kryder
1969: *The Whole World Is Watching* (TV Movie)... Officer Harry Platt
1970: *Zig Zag*... Asst. Dist. Atty. Herb Gates
1970: *Do Not Throw Cushions Into the Ring*... Christopher Belton
1971: *D.A.: Conspiracy to Kill* (TV Movie)... James Fletcher
1971: *Sweet, Sweet Rachel* (TV Movie)... Dr. Simon Tyler
1972: *Fuzz*... Det. Andy Parker
1973: *Hunter* (TV Movie)... Alain Praetorious

TELEVISION

Mannix
"Huntdown" (1967) ... Sheriff Weed
"End Game" (1969) ... Gus Keller
"To Draw the Lightning" (1972) ... Lt. Larry Gifford

189

Cade's County
1972 "Dead Past" ... Jason Benedict

The F.B.I.
"The Escape" (1966) ... Eddie Drake
"Region of Peril" (1968) ... Frank Padgett
"The Maze" (1969) ... Frank Welles
"The Prey" (1969) ... Carl S. Beaumont
"Incident in the Desert" (1970) ... John Elgin
"The Mastermind: Part 1" (1971) ... Howard Rademaker
"The Mastermind: Part 2" (1971) ... Howard Rademaker

The Young Lawyers
"Conrad and the Taxi Squad" (1971) ... Pete Pierce

Alias Smith and Jones
"Stagecoach Seven" (1971) ... Harry Downs

Bonanza
"Dead and Gone" (1965) ... Johann Brunner
"A Dream to Dream" (1968) ... Josh Carter
"Terror at 2:00" (1971) ... Mr. Ganns

Gunsmoke
"The Pariah" (1965) ... Ben Hooker
"My Father's Guitar" (1966) ... Jack
"The Mission" (1966) ... Ashe
"Noose of Gold" (1967) ... John Farron
"Exodus 21:22" (1969) ... Frank Reardon
"Jenny" (1970) ... Lucas Pritchard

The Silent Force
"Take as Directed for Death" (1970) ... Ed Stanford

Bracken's World
"Nude Scene" (1970) ... Larry Sims

Men at Law
"The Pastures of Hell" (1970) ... Rev. Neil Dana

Mod Squad
"Search and Destroy" (1970) ... Tom Blake

The Young Rebels
"Suicide Squad" (1970) ... Sgt. Nobby Whipple

Here Come the Brides
"The Soldier" (1969) ... Sgt. Noah Todd
"Absalom" (1970) ... Oliver Tray / Howard Tray

Paris 7000
"Journey to Nowhere" (1970)

Medical Center
"Fright and Flight" (1970) ... Zach Hibbs

Mission: Impossible
"The Astrologer" (1967) ... Col. Alex Stahl
"The Mind of Stefan Miklos" (1969) ... Stefan Miklos
"The Amnesiac" (1969) ... Maj. Paul Johan

Then Came Bronson
"Two Percent of Nothing: (1969) ... Royce MacLeod

The Name of the Game
"Nightmare" (1968) ... Ralph Hoak
"Chains of Command" (1969) ... Capt. Oliver

Marcus Welby, M.D.
"The Foal" (1969) ... Bob Stewart

The Bold Ones: The Lawyers
"A Game of Chance" (1969) ... Lt. William Anderson

The Virginian
"The Fatal Journey" (1963) ... Stub O'Dell
"The Hero" (1964) ... Matson
"Last Grave at Socorro Creek" (1969) ... Four-Eyes

Star Trek
"Whom Gods Destroy" (1969) ... Garth of Izar

The Outcasts
"The Night Riders" (1968) ... Jeb Collins

It Takes a Thief
"Turnabout" (1968) ... Col. Gilveney

Ironside
"The Fourteenth Runner" (1967) ... Peter Zarkov

Dundee and the Culhane
"The Catch a Thief Brief" (1967) ... Ben Murcheson

Iron Horse
"Joy Unconfined" (1966) ... Luke Joy
"The Silver Bullet" (1967) ... Ray McCoy

Cimarron Strip
"The Hunted" (1967) ... Felix Gauge

Police Story
(TV Pilot and TV movie)… Capt. James Paige

The Fugitive
"Cry Uncle" (1964) ... Officer Hasbro
"The Walls of Night" (1967) ... Art Meredith

The Felony Squad
"Target!" (1967) ... Vic Durant

Shane
"The Bitter, the Lonely" (1966) ... R.G. Posey

I Dream of Jeannie
"My Master, the Rainmaker" (1966) ... Sgt. Ben Roberts

Blue Light
"Field of Dishonor" (1966) ... Wilhelm Gerhardt

The Big Valley
"Teacher of Outlaws" (1966) ... Will

Daniel Boone
"Perilous Journey" (1965) ... Tyler

Honey West
"A Million Bucks in Anybody's Language" (1965) ... Garth

Bob Hope Presents the Chrysler Theatre
"Something About Lee Wiley" (1963) ... Dr. Matthews
"A Case of Armed Robbery" (1964) ... Steve Cortel
"Murder in the First" (1964) ... Lieutenant Malloy
"Highest Fall of All" (1965) ... Doyle Ralston

Perry Mason
"The Case of the Duplicate Case" (1965) ... Charlie Parks

Rawhide
"Retreat" (1965) ... Kaster

Profiles in Courage
"Robert A. Taft" (1965) ... Tom Smith

The Outer Limits
"The Inheritors: Part I & Part II" (1964) ... Lt. Philip Minns

Voyage to the Bottom of the Sea
"The Price of Doom" (1964) ... Pennell

Dr. Kildare
"The Hand That Hurts, the Hand That Heals" (1964) ... Dr. James
    Rothson

Slattery's People
"Question: Remember the Dark Sins of Youth?" (1964) ... Sena-
    tor Buckmaster

Death Valley Days
"The Streets of El Paso" (1964) ... Rick Hubbard

Channing
"Christmas Day Is Breaking Wan" (1964) ... Professor Roy Lucas

77 Sunset Strip
"Queen of the Cats" (1964) ... Vince

Kraft Suspense Theatre
"The Name of the Game" (1963) ... Pit Boss

Temple Houston
"Seventy Times Seven" (1963) ... Ben Wade

The Lieutenant
"A Very Private Affair" (1963) ... Major Roswell Murray

Hawaiian Eye
"Lament for a Saturday Warrior" (1962) ... Clay Barker

Day In Court
Untitled episode (1959)… (uncredited)

Highway Patrol
"Cargo Hijack" (1959) ... Joe Tyler

Flight
"The Derelict" (1958)… character unnamed

Mike Hammer
"Jury of One" (1958) ... Jack O'Dell

Mackenzie's Raiders
Untitled episode (1958)… (uncredited)

Traffic Court
Untitled episode (1957)… (uncredited)

Sources

Armstrong, Bonnie Scott. Email correspondence with the author. 2017.

Asner, Liza. Email correspondence and telephone interviews with the author. 2015 - 2018.

Asner, Ed. Telephone interview with the author, as well as written source material. 2015.

Barrett, Rona. Twitter correspondence with the author. 2015.

Bernstein, Rachel; Academy of Motion Picture Arts and Sciences, Margaret Herrick Library. Email correspondence with the author. 2016.

Birge, Daniele; Marche du Film. Email correspondence with the author. 2016.

Brittany, Morgan. Email correspondence and telephone interview with the author. 2016.

Brooks, Sandy. Email correspondence with the author. 2016 - 2017.

Carmody, Don. Email correspondence with the author. 2017.

Chicoine, Susan; The Old Globe Theatre. Email correspondence with the author. 2017.

CitizenInfo, Marseille, France. Email correspondence with the author. 2017.

Clarke, Gary. Email correspondence and telephone interviews with the author. 2015 - 2018.

Converse, Frank. Email correspondence and telephone interview with the author. 2016.

Dane, Larry. Email correspondence and telephone interview with the author. 2016.

Dawn, Melanie. Correspondence with the author. 2015.

Drury, James. Telephone interview with the author. 2015.

Duvall, Robert. Correspondence with the author. 2016.

French, Joan. Email correspondence and telephone interview with the author. 2016.

Gonzalez, Miriam; KOLO News 8 ABC. Email correspondence with the author. 2016.

Goranson, Linda. Email correspondence with the author. 2017.

Gould-Pilz, Amy. Correspondence with the author. 2017.

Grajeda, Wayne. Email correspondence with the author, as well as extensive source material. 2017 - 2018.

Gulager, Clu. Telephone interview with the author. 2016.

Gurney, Doug. Email correspondence, telephone interviews, and in-person interview with the author, as well as source material. 2017.

Hart, Susan. Email correspondence with the author. 2016.

Hoffman, Trudy. Email correspondence with the author. 2016.

Hopkins, Wendy. Email correspondence with the author. 2016.

Houghton, Margaret. Email correspondence with the author. 2015.

Hydro One Networks; Jessica. Email correspondence with the author. 2016.

Joyner, C. Courtney. Email correspondence with the author. 2016.

la Tuee, Omar. Correspondence with the author. 2017.

Les Hôtels Barrière. Email correspondence with the author. 2016.

Lodge, Steve. Email correspondence and telephone interviews with the author, as well as photos and source material. 2015 - 2017.

Mairie de Cannes. Correspondence with the author. 2017.

Makaj, Sue. Telephone interview with the author. 2015.

Makaj, Steve. Email correspondence and telephone interviews with the author. 2016 - 2018.

Marshall, Sally (Ihnat). Email correspondence, telephone and in-person interviews with the author, as well as extensive source material. 2015 - 2018.

Martinez, Dr. Raymond. Correspondence with the author. 2017.

Martinez, Vidal. Correspondence with the author. 2017.

Michel, Gaby. Email correspondence and interviews with the author. 2015 - 2017.

Mikels, Ted. Email interviews with the author. 2016.

Minsky, Juliana. Email correspondence with the author. 2016.

Mordue, Emily. Email correspondence and interviews with the author. 2015 - 2016.

Mordue-Humphries, Brenda. Email correspondence, telephone and in-person interviews with the author, as well as extensive source material. 2015 - 2018.

Osifchin, Steven. Email correspondence with the author. 2015 - 2017.

Peterson, Barbara. Email correspondence with the author. 2015.

Poggiali, Chris. Email correspondence with the author. 2016.

Rzemienski, Gloria and Wally. Email correspondence with the author. 2016 - 2018.

Schuck, John. Email correspondence with the author. 2016.

Simon, Jeff; Buffalo [NY] News. Email correspondence with the author. 2016.

United States Consulate General, Marseille, France. Email correspondence with the author. 2017.

Valtenbergs, Ed. Email correspondence with the author. 2016.

Woods, Grahame. Email correspondence with the author. 2017.

Writers Guild of America West. Email correspondence with the author. 2017.

Books

Weaver, Tom. 2005. *Earth Vs. The Sci-fi Filmmakers: Twenty Interviews.* McFarland & Company, Inc.

Etter, Jonathan. *Gangway, Lord! (The) Here Comes The Brides Book.* BearManor Media.

Newspapers

Abilene Reporter-News [TX]
Albuquerque Tribune [NM]
Anderson Daily Bulletin [IN]
Berkshire Eagle [MA]
Big Spring Herald [TX]
Brownsville Herald [TX]
Colorado Springs Gazette Telegraph [CO]
Corpus Christi Caller-Times [TX]
Courier-Express [PA]
Courier-Journal [KY]
Daily Reporter [OH]
Decatur Daily Review [IL]
Des Moines Register [IA]
El Paso Herald [TX]
Evening Review [OH]

Florida Today [FL]
Grand Prairie Daily News [TX]
Hamilton Spectator [Canada]
Herald-Mail [MD]
Independent Press Telegram [CA]
Independent Star-News [CA]
Index-Journal [SC]
Kingston Daily Freeman [NY]
Lawton Constitution [OK]
Los Angeles Times [CA]
Monroe News-Star [LA]
Mountaineer [Canada]
News Journal [DE]
Oil City Derrick [PA]
Oklahoma City Daily Oklahoman [OK]
Ottawa Citizen [Canada]
Ottawa Journal [Canada]
Paris News [TX]
Philadelphia Inquirer [PA]
Pittsburgh Press [PA]
Post-Crescent [WI]
San Antonio Express [TX]
Sheboygan Press [WI]
Standard-Speaker [PA]
Star News [CA]
Sydney Morning Herald [Australia]
Tennessean [TN]
Times Record [NY]
Tipton Daily Tribune [IN]
Toronto Daily Star [Canada]
Toronto Telegram [Canada]
Valley Morning Star [TX]
Washington Post [DC]
Winona Daily News [MN]

Magazines and Periodicals
TV Guide
Variety

Columnists and Nationally-Syndicated Writers

Bawden, James. "TV & Radio"
Grace, Roger M. "REMINISCING - TV Courtroom Shows Proliferate in the Late 1950s"
Hocura, Ed.
Miller, Jack. "TV & Radio"
"TV Scout Reports"

Websites

http://www.tccweb.org
http://www.volcanoseven.com
http://www.metnews.com/articles/reminiscing050803.htm
https://tarlton.law.utexas.edu/exhibits/mason_&_associates/documents/reality_series_by_title.pdf
http://www.imdb.com
http://wearecontrollingtransmission.blogspot.com/2011/03/inheritors-parts-1-2.html
http://home.earthlink.net/~markholcomb/ol/ol_inheritors.html
http://www.tcm.com/this-month/article/410112|0/Kona-Coast.html
http://moviemorlocks.com/2011/08/18/joan-blondell-goes-hawaiian
http://www.truewestmagazine.com/bull-doggin
https://www.tapatalk.com/groups/monsterkidclassichorrorforum/gary-clarke-s-early-movies-and-steve-ihnat-t25274.html#.VsOTZeZ1eDm
http://templeofschlock.blogspot.com/2009/07/round-table-discussion-you-and-me-and.html
http://mcmolo.blogspot.com/2013/08/captains-blog-pt-55-whom-gods-destroy.html
http://richardkimblethefugitive.com/fugitivescreencaps117.htm

About the Author

LINDA ALEXANDER GREW UP starry-eyed as an avid consumer of television and movies in the 1970s. After doing the hustle and watching *The Mod Squad*, she began writing about entertainment characters who engaged her imagination. She has written for magazines and newspapers, with many articles and books to her credit. She appeared on *The Oprah Show*. As a forever student of human nature, many personalities lives in her head 24/7, forever talking to her. She always talks back, and conversations are always entertaining.

Her books include biographies on Golden Era movie star, Robert Taylor; TV's Maverick brother, Jack Kelly; and the voice of the talking TV horse, Mister Ed, and movie serial cowboy, Allan "Rocky" Lane, all published by BearManor Media. Her newest release is the biography of arguably the busiest guest star actor on television in the 1960s and 1970s, *The Life and Death of Rising Star Steve Ihnat—Gone Too Soon*.

Index